Our House of The Sacred Heart

A Litany of Stories with Art, Prayers, Poetry and Reflections toward Consecration to the Sacred Heart

Annabelle Moseley

En Route Books and Media, LLC
St. Louis, MO

ENROUTE
Make the time

En Route Books and Media
5705 Rhodes Ave., St. Louis, MO, 63109

Contact us at contactus@enroutebooksandmedia.com
Copyright © 2021 Annabelle Moseley
Cover Design by TJ Burdick

Hardback ISBN: 978-1-952464-44-7
Paperback ISBN: 978-1-952464-43-0
E-Book ISBN: 978-1-952464-45-4
Library of Congress Control Number: 2020952399

All poems featured in *Our House of the Sacred Heart* are original works of art written by Annabelle Moseley. Images of art are in the public domain. The beautiful art of the Seminary of the Immaculate Conception in Huntington, New York is mostly "artist unknown" and thus not attributed.

Contents

Our House of the Sacred Heart...........5

Preface...........7

Dedication...........27

    A Sonnet Crown for the Sacred Heart...........29

The Twelve Promises of the Sacred Heart of Jesus...........33

A Litany of Lessons...........35

    The Dogwood...........37

    The Shoes...........45

    The Wave...........53

    The Gifts...........59

    The Garbage...........69

    The Palms...........77

    The Bow...........85

    The Paperweight...........91

    The Hands...........101

    The Queen Anne's Lace...........109

    The Magnolias...........117

    The Clocks...........125

    The Door...........133

    The Psalmist...........143

    The Blue Willow Plates...........151

    The Kitchen...........159

    The Bethany Cook...........179

    The Birchbark...........187

    The Arched Window...........197

    The Cemetery...........205

    The Sand Dollar...........213

    The Statue...........223

    The Dove...........233

      The Golden Chapel of the Sacred Heart...........241

    The Book...........255

    The Birth Offering...........263

    The Peacock Pin...........271

    The Elevator...........281

The Sage's Blessing...291
The Child's Blessing...307
The Last Labor..317
The Renovation...325
The Song...335
The New House of the Sacred Heart............................343
Enthronement of Your Home to the Sacred Heart of Jesus
....355
Afterword: The Starry Mantle.......................................359
The Litany of the Sacred Heart of Jesus.......................367
About the Author..370

Our House of the Sacred Heart

"In peace I will lie down and sleep, for you alone, Lord, make me dwell in safety" –Psalm 4:8

In our house of the Sacred Heart,
from which we're called to never part,
there are mysteries of joy and pain—
where the warmest days bring the hardest rain;
at life's truest moments, it is there we have lain.

There is family in our house of the Sacred Heart
who have taught us the meaning of a blessed day.
Their journeys cross ours— and point the way.
Ancestors, saints, family and friends—
pray for us till this journey ends.

This house is the place we'll always keep
The memories that never sleep—
The poignant love that runs so deep.
Each of us has rested our head
in trust upon our God and Bread.

In our house of the Sacred Heart,
from which we're called to never part,
there are mysteries of joy and pain—
where the warmest days bring the hardest rain;
at life's truest moments, it is there we have lain.

"One thing I ask from the Lord, this only do I seek: that I may dwell in the house of the Lord all the days of my life, to gaze on the beauty of the Lord and to seek him in his temple. For in the day of trouble he will keep me safe in his dwelling; he will hide me in the shelter of his sacred tent and set me high upon a rock." –Psalm 27:4-5

"God Appears to Abraham"
James Tissot

Preface

I. Reparation to The Sacred Heart

"But he was pierced for our offenses, crushed for our sins; Upon him was the chastisement that makes us whole, by his stripes we were healed... Though he had done no wrong nor spoken any falsehood." –Isa 53:5-9

St. Augustine wrote, "You have made us for yourself, O Lord, and our hearts are restless until they rest in Thee." I pray that this book will remind each of us, myself included, that we find rest in the Sacred Heart of Jesus... the true home of each of our hearts. The Sacred Heart remains vulnerable to abuse in this world even as it vulns for our sake.

In medieval times, the image of the pelican mother piercing her own breast to feed her starving chicks with her blood was an image of Jesus' Eucharistic Heart known as "the pelican in her piety," and the word given for that action was "vulning" from which the word, vulnerable comes. The "Vulnerary of Christ" refers to the Five Wounds that Jesus Christ suffered at the Crucifixion: their symbolism and representation in religious art, liturgical objects, etc. Jesus and the saints remind anyone who loves deeply, of the worthwhile price of sacrificial love: vulnerability.

There is a colloquial expression: "wearing one's heart on one's sleeve." In every image of the Sacred Heart, what is so poignant is how Jesus points to His revealed and unprotected

Heart, leaving Himself vulnerable out of His desire to give His Heart to us and to receive ours in return. Yet on the day of this writing, I read in the news about the desecration of a statue of the Sacred Heart of Jesus in a church in Texas; the statue was shattered and broken. This sacrilege has only given me more desire to press forward with this book and hope that my writing of it and those who read it might, in doing so, offer love and reparation to that same unguarded heart that is held out to us in the hand of our Lord. There is no doubt that the work of evil is rampant in the world today; we see shocking signs of it everywhere. Let us all join in an act of reparation through praying the Litany of the Sacred Heart of Jesus as stories, art and reflections unfold in Our House of the Sacred Heart.

The family is the heart of the culture of life. The philosopher Pliny the Elder famously stated, "home is where the heart is". But whose heart? It is the Sacred Heart which must always reign as monarch there, and in fact, be the eternal home from which our earthly one forms its beat.

II. Refuge in the Sacred Heart

"You who dwell in the shelter of the Most High, who abide in the shadow of the Almighty, Say to the Lord, My refuge and my fortress, my God in whom I trust." –Psalm 91:1-2

S imply put, the Sacred Heart is our home. This book will share stories of a red house that provided a concrete metaphor for this reality. It was the house of my grandparents, and it was a refuge in difficult times. The way the house was decorated and the faith-filled people who lived in and visited it gave such consolation that it was as though, within that fire-red house, I was really being embraced and sheltered by the

Sacred Heart of Jesus. Through the graces I encountered in that home and through my grandparents, parents, aunts and uncles who came and went from it like its life-blood, I have come to understand that our true home, no matter what befalls us, is the Heart of Jesus. It's your home, too.

Is it any wonder that in our Catholic faith there is a long-standing tradition of doing an Enthronement ceremony that makes Jesus the King of our home, that blesses the house and family by having an image of the Sacred Heart of Jesus displayed for veneration within the home? That ceremony is included, along with a treasury of prayers including a Consecration prayer to the Sacred Heart, in this book. Enthrone your home to the Sacred Heart. In so doing, you will bring many blessings to your family. Consecrate yourself to the Sacred Heart and offer your heart to Him for a dwelling-place. In so doing, you will bring joy to your heart and His.

In fact, although Our House of the Sacred Heart can be read at any pace the reader wishes (even in one sitting!), it can also be approached one lesson per day: a 33-day Consecration to the Sacred Heart of Jesus through a Litany of 33 Lessons. Each day's lesson includes reflection questions, and a beautiful prayer to the Sacred Heart. We are praying the Litany of the Sacred Heart together while reading this work of reparation, one lesson at a time. At book's end, there is a Consecration to the Sacred Heart of Jesus. Please note that if you skip a day leading to the consecration, do not worry... just make it up the next day.

If you wish to read this book as one lesson per day, culminating in your consecration, you may start anytime, as anytime is a great time to draw closer to the Sacred Heart! If you wish to consecrate yourself on the Feast of the Sacred Heart that would be very special, indeed. But as the feast of the Sacred Heart of Jesus is one of the so-called "Movable Feasts," occurring on a different date each year, you'll need to find the date for the feast in the year you're starting and count 33 days before to begin. But again, any time is a wonderful time to consecrate yourself to the Sacred Heart of Jesus!

However it is read, the stories in this book can be returned to time and again, for each of the 33 Lessons is a unique, true story of a living devotion to the Sacred Heart as handed down through five generations, and layered with art, scripture, poems and devotions. Our House of the Sacred Heart is a spiritual autobiography showing growth in the Faith transiting the various gateways of life. Best of all, the book teaches you, the reader, to discover your own spiritual autobiography, as well.

St. Vincent de Paul was a saint devoted to the Sacred Heart of Jesus. This was the coin given to my grandfather, for founding his parish St. Vincent de Paul Society.

"Lord of Charity"
St. Louise de Merillac
Devotee of the Sacred Heart, and
friend of St. Vincent de Paul

"Sacred Heart of Jesus Surrounded by Angels, with St. Ignatius of
Loyola and St. Louis Gonzaga"
José de Paez

III. Becoming a Student of Grace

"The task the Lord Jesus has given me is – the task of testifying to the good news of God's grace" –Acts 20:24

When I was a child, you could say I became a student of grace. This goal might sound lofty or high, and it might seem like the kind of thing that doesn't help at all when things get tough. On the contrary, it is practical and essential and if you practice it in ordinary time, day to day, when you are called to handle some great challenge, it will get you through. I speak from experience. You have probably been a student of grace, too, whether you've ever thought of it that way or not, and if not; well, you're being called now.

The Catechism of the Catholic Church defines grace as, "favour, the free and undeserved help that God gives us to respond to His call to become children of God, adoptive children, partakers of the divine nature and of eternal life." And so grace is free, undeserved help that enables us to respond to our calling to help build and dwell forever in God's Kingdom. How was I a student of that grace? Though my family was certainly not perfect and each of us are mere sinners hoping to turn into saints... the striving, the working, and the loving that I observed in each of them at the Red House made me want to become a builder of what I was a witness to there, and dwell forever in the place its strong foundation and humble walls anticipated: the Sacred Heart.

My grandfather was one of the founders of our parish St. Vincent de Paul Society, a group whose focus is to provide aid to the poor and needy of the parish and surrounding neighborhoods. Central to the teachings of St. Vincent de Paul is a love of Jesus's Heart. St. Vincent de Paul wrote, "May Our

Lord be in our hearts and our hearts in His." A powerful way to Christ's heart is taking care of the poor. *"The King will say... 'Truly I say to you, to the extent that you did it to one of the least of these brothers of Mine, you did it to Me.'"* MT 25:40.

My grandmother had served as President of the Rosary Society in our parish. She was particularly drawn to the Sorrowful Mysteries, invoking Jesus when she was suffering, joining hers to His. When she would go for painful monthly eye shots to help delay the effects of macular degeneration, her prayer was this: "Be with me, Lord, when I am in trouble and need." In her younger days, she often attended the Wednesday night Holy Hour of Reparation to the Sacred Heart.

It is said in Scripture that *"by their fruits shall you know them"* MT 7:15. My grandparents' fruits, their children, were all people of faith and they came in and out of the "Red House" like its life's blood. Visits from them were plentiful and I witnessed these vibrant aunts and uncles, each with their own unique attributes and a bond of prayerfulness, introspection, and integrity of faith, balanced with humor and good cheer. They gleamed with joy in the Lord as they were all raised within the Red House and had learned their lessons well. From my frequent seat in the bay window of the kitchen, my spirits would rise when I'd see one of their cars pull up in front of the white picket fence and a smiling aunt or uncle emerge and wave. For the only child I was, their presence in my life was a treasured grace. My mother made their gifts and struggles come alive for me through so many stories of their growing-up, and I memorized the family lore she shared with more interest than a gripping book. Although my mother and her five siblings all lived in different parishes, they frequently came together, over the decades, to worship in their home parish where my grandparents were pillars. How often two whole pews would be filled with the strong, devoted children they had raised. My grandmother would say how graced she was to have

Preface

her children's busy paths connect on so many Sundays – together to share the Lord's Supper, each receiving the Sacred Heart of Jesus through the Most Holy Eucharist, and the special graces given therein.

We witness God's grace on our life's transfiguring mountains. But it's also there, even in the storm before the fourth watch of the night, the kind of storm I took refuge from in the Red House. It was there I learned that when things are at their darkest, when we can't hear God's voice over the wind, we can train our ears to listen for the sound of the Sacred Whisper. My grandparents' house was the beating heart of the family even during our storms. There were discussions of faith, and frequent family stories of the brave generations before. I learned my family's story and studied the recurring pattern, as in Scripture: those who triumphed did so through faith and sacrifice – every time.

Grace is granted when we pray and request it, and it helps when we can train our eye to recognize it – to be attentive to the clues left by God in each of our lives. It is what I call the gift of the poet's eye, and it was this gift that allowed me to accept those graces. This gift, honed over the years and joined to faith, saved me at critical times of great loss, when I could have easily taken another path, losing my way and missing the clues that were there all the time, like life rafts – that are there for all of us – if we can just cultivate that vision to see them. The poet's eye can make beauty out of mess and pain – and see something numinous in the ordinary. I want to train your eye to see the poetry in your life – the poetry of God the Word made Flesh and the Author of Salvation, whose very life was the most perfect poem.

Whatever your story, however painful, be assured that God has left signs and symbols along the way–clues to guide you to his heart. I want this book to allow you see the clues I have come to see—that God leaves—to teach each of us lessons. Like the Dogwood blossom where the wounds of Christ are present on a beautiful flower, hidden in plain sight, there are clues of God's great Mysteries and Graces left throughout our lives: in nature; in the goodness of others; in lovely music and art; even in ordinary household objects or tasks. But take caution: as CS Lewis reminds: "The books or the music in which we thought the beauty was located will betray us if we trust to them; it was not in them, it only came through them, and what came through them was longing. These things—the beauty, the memory of our own past—are good images of what we really desire; but if they are mistaken for the thing itself they turn into dumb idols, breaking the hearts of their worshipers. For they are not the thing itself; they are only the scent of a flower we have not found, the echo of a tune we have not heard, news from a country we have never yet visited." And that country is Heaven. All the good things we love in this world are just calling us to praise the beauty of God and to anticipate Heaven. The clues He leaves us can lead us there.

There is a Ponder & Pray section at the end of every lesson in this book to help you reflect upon your own life story of faith and family. I reiterate: *Whatever your story*, God has left signs and symbols along the way. May this book help you to cultivate the vision to see those signs more clearly, like a map of your life story unfolding.

"The Storm on the Sea of Galilee"
Rembrandt van Rijn

IV. A Legendary House

"As for me and my house, we will serve the Lord."
–Josh 24:15

During our family's most sorrowful and luminous mysteries, I found myself in the Red House more than my own, eating there multiple times a week, and even living there for a time. The Red House belonged to my grandfather, "Grandpapa," and grandmother, "Nanabelle."

Grandpapa's parents were immigrants. He was the fourth of five children born to Irish and Scotch-English immigrants. His mother, a well-educated teacher in Ireland, could only find a governess position in America. Among her few treasured belongings was her favorite book: a well-worn copy of "Jesus, the Master Teacher" by Herman Horne. Widowed young, she was known for waking each morning with the sweet words, "Thanks be to God for this blessed day!" My grandfather had only one vivid memory of his dad: playing hide-and-seek every night as his father walked in from work. He waited in some well-chosen place to be found by his dad with a joyful embrace. His father died when Grandpapa was only six, and I believe I saw that lingering sadness in him, not knowing that I, too, would experience grief in my youth.

Nanabelle also had an early loss. She was the second of ten children born to deeply faithful Catholic parents. Her young brother died when she was six. She and her older brother, T., who became a priest, shared that sorrow their whole lives. It bonded them in a very deep and spiritual way. I believe the mirror experience of confronting the trauma of death so early in my grandparents' lives brought a unique understanding between them of what is important in life and how they would raise their children.

How may I begin to describe their legendary house— outside, it was painted a deep fire-red, like the color of the Sacred Heart, and it was a pulsing thrum of life to the many who entered, with a white picket fence out front; surrounded by roses and thorns.

Cowbells clattered with rollicking joy when you opened the door, no matter the season or mood in which you found yourself. The rooms were filled with whimsical antiques and classic religious art. In the Living Room, over the piano was the Holy Family depicted on the "Flight into Egypt" by George Hitchcock, a painting in blue and white tones of Our Lady cradling the Christ child close, fleeing on the donkey, with St. Joseph walking behind them, allowing them to be first and foremost in the scene, and to protect and guard them from marauders who might attack from behind. The scene was covered with Queen Anne's Lace, a significant flower for my grandmother, mother, and I who were all named "after beautiful Saint Anne." It was as though St. Anne was somehow present in the scene, journeying with her daughter, reminding Mary of her love with each lacy bloom in the wild field. The painting signified the steady love of parents: a father willing to sacrifice for his family, and a mother comforting her child at every step of the journey.

Upon the piano was a carved wooden statue of St. Joseph the Worker, wearing a carpenter's apron and holding the tools of his trade, reminding the family of the value of hard work without complaint and of steady strength in the face of challenges. Also in the living room was a gold-framed still-life of a red flower. If you looked closely, the petals were heart-shaped.

There was a large crucifix with a bronze Corpus, so large that it was obvious how paramount devotion to their Redeemer was to my grandparents. There was a framed embroidery proclaiming, "Life is Fragile... Handle with Prayer." And there was a tapestry that reminded: "Home is where the heart is" with a large red heart at its center. The bookcase was filled with religious and devotional classics, prayer-books and missals. One of my favorites had the Sacred Heart of Jesus on the cover, and prayers to his Divine Heart within. Featured in a prominent part of the home, the high stairwell wall leading from the first floor to the second, was a black and white painting of Jesus, with a suffering but handsome face, prominent crown of thorns and beautiful Sacred Heart. For the children who grew up in that house, their image of Jesus was impacted by their daily climb up the stairs, where they'd pause a moment to look up at their Savior and make sure their shoulders hadn't tilted the frame as they ascended the stairs to bed.

The kitchen was always ready to welcome whomever dropped by. I used to watch the care with which my grandmother prepared a meal; the way she always made more than she needed in case someone in the family stopped by unexpectedly (and someone often did); the way she always set a table with great attention to detail even for a simple meal. The food was served on her signature blue willow plates. Each night, I watched the thoughtful way my grandfather prepared the table in advance for the next day's breakfast, setting out spoons and bowls and coffee cups with a monk's discipline. It ensured that no matter how early I awoke, a place had already been prepared for me at the table. Our family's patriarch and matriarch had servants' hearts.

One of the greatest epic poems is The Odyssey. The hero, Odysseus, learns after his journeys to both harrowing and enticing locales, that the most important journey is the one home. It's one of the richest discoveries we can make: our eternal home in Heaven is the end-goal. To quote St. Therese of Lisieux, "The world's thy ship and not thy home." And yet a noble quest in this life is to make an epic place to live that reminds one of Heaven; neither a house impressive for the sake of impressing, nor merely a convenient place to hang your hat, but a dwelling place so filled with goodness and meaning, that anyone who enters can feel something special there, and long to return.

It is a worthy ambition to pray for the grace to make a home that on its humble scale — anticipates Heaven. The most ideal house that has ever been and ever will be is the home of the Holy Family, in which Jesus' Sacred Heart resided from birth to adulthood. A picture of, or prayer to the Holy Family displayed prominently in the home can remind those who dwell within of the gold standard. This book contains a compendium of prayers, reflections, and suggestions to make your house a House of the Sacred Heart.

Over the years, as I taught Graduate Theology classes, my students have always remarked about how much they loved my family stories – the cast of characters and the unusual themes I shared. But I have come to understand that in the Red House, I was really being held and forged all the time within the Sacred Heart of Jesus, our true Home, yours and mine, which does not fade or crumble with the passing of time. May we all come to be certain of that. "*In love, he predestined us to be adopted... through Jesus Christ, in accordance with his pleasure and will.*" (Eph 1:5) Together, in his heart, we are all family. As Our Lord taught us, "*In my Father's house there are many mansions... I go to prepare a place for you.*" (Jn 14:2) A friend of mine recently said, "when I think about all the good people from your family and mine who are in Heaven with God... I just can't wait!" How many people have you heard say that? It certainly resounded with me as I shaped this book.

"The Holy Family"
Juan Simón Gutiérrez

V. An Invitation

Abraham "lifted up his eyes, and looked: and lo, three men stood by him, and when he saw them, he ran to meet them from the tent door, and bowed himself to the ground. And he said, Lord, if I have now found favor in thy sight, go not, I pray thee, from thy servant. Let a little water, I pray you, be brought, and wash your feet, and rest yourselves under the tree. And I will bring a morsel of bread, that you may comfort your hearts, afterward ye shall go your ways: for therefore are ye come to your servant. And they said, Do even as thou hast said." –Gen 18:2-5

This book, with its two covers reminding of foundation and roof, is a kind of home. Every book is meant to be, I believe, though not every book... or house, either nourishes or welcomes. It is always by the grace of God. And so I ask that the Word of God made flesh, the Author of Salvation, may inspire me in my efforts to welcome you into the home of this book, and more importantly, into the true House of the Sacred Heart.

Through Him, I hope and pray that the words in between these covers will offer you hospitality. I realize that in welcoming you in, dear reader, I may be "entertaining angels unaware." Scripture reminds, *"Do not forget to entertain strangers, for by so doing some have unwittingly entertained angels"* (Heb 13:2), and I ask Our Lord, that as you read, it may be as though your feet have been washed and anointed, and you have been given a cool drink of water and a meal, with the kind of hospitality Abraham gave his three guests. And so, come on in and rest awhile and I'll tell you a story of the Red House that I have come to call Our House of the Sacred Heart.

I invite you through this book to join my family who spent time in the House of the Sacred Heart.

Come visit the unforgettable Red House, with kitchen conversations over cups of tea, rest in rocking chairs; and laughter and joy in time spent together. A Litany of Lessons is about to unfold. Each Lesson in the House of the Sacred Heart will close with one of the 33 lines from the Litany of the Sacred Heart of Jesus that invokes one of the titles of the Heart of Jesus, followed by: "have mercy on us." That way you'll be praying along with the litany, even as you read. There's a place for you at the table as the lessons and litany unfold.

The seat I offer you is in a bay window, in a kitchen with dark wide-plank wooden floors. There are country baskets hanging from the beam of the kitchen ceiling. On the antique black and white iron stove is a savory meal. The pot roast smells good, and steaming mashed potatoes are just waiting to be formed into a crater for gravy. There is an old Regulator clock on the wall to your right, next to a hutch displaying Depression-era glassware and blue and white china: a reminder of both times of scarcity and plenty. There's a rocker under the clock, and it is guaranteed to creak when you sit in it. Many times, when I sat in that kitchen, my heart was breaking. I knew death and loss, loneliness and pain from a very early age. Because the kitchen was rooted in faith and family, purpose came from my pain; gratitude arose from loss, and joy was ever-palpable within Our House of the Sacred Heart: our true home.

May we all come to be certain of our true home, and so "*lay up for ourselves treasures in heaven, where neither moth nor rust destroys and where thieves do not break in and steal. For where our treasure is, there our hearts will be also"* (Matt 6:20-21). God bless you, dear reader.

"O most Sacred, most loving Heart of Jesus, Thou art concealed in the Holy Eucharist, and Thou beatest for us still." —Saint John Henry Cardinal Newman

Dedication

I began writing this book on The Feast of the Sacred Heart June 19, 2020.

To Our Lord, Jesus Christ, the Word Made Flesh and Author of Salvation, with Devotion to His Sacred Heart

Cor ad cor loquitur

Through love, we seek to honor Your Sacred Heart. We honor Your crown of thorns, our Savior. We tend Your wounds; and give You a crown of love: prayer-flowers of thornless roses, jewels from our hearts to Yours.

Jesu mitis et humilis Corde, fac cor nostrum secundum Cor Tuum

Jesus meek and humble of Heart, make our hearts like unto Thine

"The Infant Christ with a floral wreath"
Carlo Dolci

A Sonnet Crown for the Sacred Heart

They didn't know that they had crowned a king
who oyster-like, could turn grit into pearl,
transform a thorn-crown to a royal ring—
garlands of life made from a twisted swirl.
They did not understand that He could shape
healing from hatred, blessing from a curse.
Clothed in His sacrifice, He wore the cape
they draped on Him to mock, to wound Him worse—
a blood-red cloak of pain; a rose in rain.
Seventy thorns entered His vine-draped head,
trespassed the veins of thought branching His brain.
Matting His hair, new buds sprung, where He bled.
Each thorn, upon its entrance, recognized
the mind of its creator, paradise.

Our House of the Sacred Heart

The mind of its creator: paradise—
each thorn, upon its entrance, recognized.
Matting His hair, new buds sprung, where He bled,
trespassed the veins of thought branching His brain.
Seventy thorns entered His vine-draped head.
A blood-red cloak of pain— a rose in rain
they draped on Him to mock, to wound Him worse.
Clothed in His sacrifice, He wore the cape:
healing from hatred, blessing from a curse.
They did not understand that He could shape
garlands of life made from a twisted swirl,
transform a thorn crown to a royal ring
that oyster-like, could turn grit into pearl.
They didn't know that they had crowned a king.

They didn't know that they had crowned a king,
but we do. Let our love remove the thorns—
our sacrifices, works assuage their sting,
our reparation comfort where he mourns.
We give our rosaries, and from each bud,
each decade of prayer-flowers, wind a crown
of thornless roses, red, as though our blood
is offered up. Let each of us dig down
and garden our soul for love of Him.
Let's make a new crown for Him out of love,
mine jewels within our hearts, raised like a hymn
we lift them up, offer to Him above.
Let us withhold nothing from Him and lift
a new crown for the One who mends the rift.

A Sonnet Crown for the Sacred Heart

A new crown for the One who mends the rift
between mankind and God. What can we mend?
What can we give our Savior as a gift—
what comfort and what healing can we send?
Through prayer, let us smooth myrrh into His palms,
soothe His right hand, which pointed to His heart,
hammered in Joseph's workshop, un-scrolled psalms
within the Temple, made mercy an art.
We lift the left hand now, and wipe the blood
from the nail mark, this hand patted the head
of child after child, formed the mud
into a healing poultice He would spread
upon the blind man's eyes. We were all blind.
See His wounds? Let us wash them. Let us bind.

See His wounds? Let us wash them. Let us bind.
Through prayer we bend to wash both His pierced feet
smooth myrrh— a gift the Magi left behind
for just this moment— make each gash replete
with ointment. These feet walked the Holy Land
held up the Light, the Door, the Vine, God's Son,
the Son of Man, and moved him, let him stand.
With perfume and with tears, anoint each one.
His body now takes such a different form.
Securely binding every outstretched limb,
wrapping with linen cloth to keep Him warm,
we work, through prayer, to minister to Him.
We praise God for our Savior's feet and hands,
His heart that loves us, mind that understands.

His heart that loves us, mind that understands—
We also praise God for our Savior's side.
Pierced by a lance, it spilled upon the lands
of every time and place, a holy tide
of mercy. Blood and water flowed. We touch
His side, as Doubting Thomas felt the gash
that mercifully brought belief. This clutch
of certainty returned fire to ash—
brought zeal to lukewarm doubt.
This side of Christ was often embraced by
his mother's arms, circled about
each time he'd bid his sweet Mother goodbye.
We praise God for Christ's sacrificial side
"Within His Holy Wounds we fain would hide."

"Within His Holy Wounds we fain would hide."
And now, we sing His Sacred Heart, the flame
atop of it that has intensified
with love— the fire that knows us each by name.
We sing the cross atop the heart, each thorn
encircling it like a saving chain,
and binding us to him. Now we adorn
His heart with prayer. We celebrate its reign—
align our clock-like pulse to know His beat.
The ones who mocked Him didn't know His heart,
or that He could turn rot to something sweet;
they didn't know He had mastered the art—
that out of pain, he'd make a royal ring.
They didn't know that they had crowned a king.

The Twelve Promises of the Sacred Heart of Jesus

These twelve promises of the Sacred Heart of Jesus were given to St. Margaret Mary by Our Lord in his appearances to her between 1673-1675. These promises have been approved by the Church. The promises apply to those who respond to the call of the Sacred Heart to return His love. In the words of St. Margaret Mary, "I do not know of any other exercise in the spiritual life that is more calculated to raise a soul in a short amount of time to the height of perfection and to make it taste the true sweetness to be found in the service of Jesus Christ."

1. I will give them all the graces necessary in their state of life.

2. I will establish peace in their homes.

3. I will comfort them in all their afflictions.

4. I will be their secure refuge during life, and above all, in death.

5. I will bestow abundant blessings upon all their undertakings.

6. Sinners will find in My Heart the source and infinite ocean of mercy.

7. Lukewarm souls shall become fervent.

8. Fervent souls shall quickly mount to high perfection.

9. I will bless every place in which an image of My Heart is exposed and honored.

10. I will give to priests the gift of touching the most hardened hearts.

11. Those who shall promote this devotion shall have their names written in My Heart.

12. I promise you in the excessive mercy of My Heart that My all powerful love will grant to all those who receive Holy Communion on the First Fridays in nine consecutive months the grace of final perseverance; they shall not die in My disgrace, nor without receiving their sacraments. My divine Heart shall be their safe refuge in this last moment.

"Sacred Heart of Jesus with Angel and St. Margaret Mary Alacoque" from the Seminary of the Immaculate Conception

A Litany of Lessons

"The ordinary acts we practice every day at home are of more importance to the soul than their simplicity might suggest."
–St. Thomas More

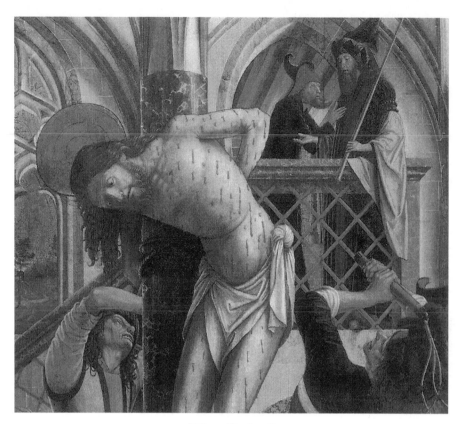

"Flagellation"
Michael Facher

The Lesson of The Dogwood

"The Lord God gave man this order: you are free to eat from any of the trees of the garden except the tree of knowledge of good and evil; from that tree you shall not eat." –Gen 2:16-17

"The Thorn"
James Hayllar

The Dogwood

Flowers bearing the scars of Christ were not
to pick, you said. Soft white with crimson red
like spots of blood— stigma like a thorn crown
at the center of the bloom—
our fingers weren't worthy
of the touch. A lavish restraint—
rooted from a memory of Eden.
All the same— how much your reverence
must have pleased the Lord,
whose tree of sacrifice awaits—
restored— in paradise.

Our House of the Sacred Heart

At the Red House of my grandparents, there was a narrow, white picket gate atop a small hill that connected the neighbors' homes, so they could visit easily. One day, when I was six, I walked hand-in-hand with my grandfather on an errand to that neighbor, to drop off a tool for his garden. As we descended the hill, we passed beneath the white and pink canopy of a flowering dogwood tree. I reached up and picked a blossom of a low-hanging branch and began to twirl it.

"No, dear. You must never pick a dogwood blossom," my grandfather said. "The dogwood flower bears the wounds of Christ." He had me look more closely at what I'd seen as just a flower. Now, I could see the blood stains on each petal, the crown of thorns at the center. I was struck at finding a reminder of Christ's crucifixion in the beauty of nature. A message of the Father's sacrifice for us had been imprinted by Him on this tree, with the wounds of His Son in plain sight, yet easily missed to the casual glance. I vowed then and there to never pick the dogwood's blossom. My mind vibrant with images from my Children's illustrated Picture Bible, I recognized that this was a discipline akin to the command God gave Adam and Eve regarding the Tree of the Knowledge of Good and Evil. My grandfather, the one who had always tended the wounds and removed the splinters I'd gotten in his yard had shown me our garden's untouchable fruit and I, out of love, would obey.

Looking back, I see a poetic strand in my grandfather's soul like Gerard Manley Hopkins, who saw the world "charged with the grandeur of God." Dogwood Hill was no Mount Moriah or Mount Tabor, but I did learn a powerful lesson there, a rule, to see God in nature; to put God first even in the little things; and to love him lavishly by resisting a fairly innocuous impulse to pick a pretty bloom. I had been given a child's law of love, and was never quite the same.

Ponder and Pray

- For many of us, so much of how we learn to love and accept God's love for us comes from those we love in childhood. What adults influenced your faith when you were a child? Who influenced your faith later in life?

- Where do you see God in nature?

- **Let us pray** The Prayer of St. Gertrude to the Sacred Heart

Hail, Sacred Heart of Jesus, living and strengthening source of eternal life, infinite treasury of the divinity, burning furnace of divine love! You are my refuge and my sanctuary. My loving Savior, consume my heart in that burning fire with which Your own is inflamed. Pour into my soul those graces which flow from Your love. Let my heart be so united with Yours that our wills may be one, and my will in all things conformed with Your Will. May Your Will be the guide and rule of my desires and of my actions.

Amen.

Most holy Heart of Jesus, fountain of every blessing, I love You. With a lively sorrow for my sins I offer You this poor heart of mine. Make me humble, patient, and pure, and perfectly obedient to Your Will.

Amen.

Heart of Jesus, Son of the Eternal Father, have mercy on us.

"Christ the King"
Charles Bosseron Chambers

"Christ Washing the Feet of His Disciples" (detail)
Jacopo Tintoretto

The Lesson of The Shoes

"As your lips have instructed me, I have kept the way of the law. My steps have kept to your paths; my feet have not faltered." –Psalm 17:4-5

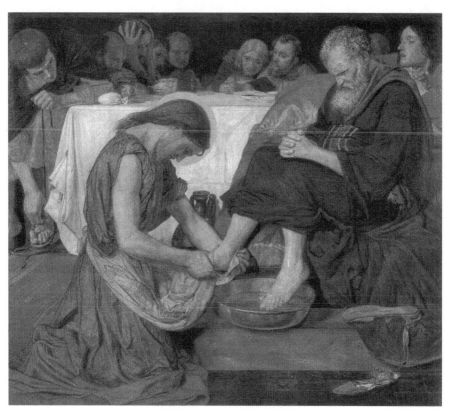

"Jesus Washing Peter's Feet"
Ford Madox Brown

Polishing the Wingtips

At night, my grandfather
would get his kit
to shine his wing-tip shoes.
He'd brush and buff,
polish and smooth.
And while he'd work, he'd sit
in his rocker and pray–
a discipline to clean
the soul, as though he knew
the place he stood upon
was holy ground
as he reached
through prayer
for grace.

My grandfather almost always wore a tie. He ironed his shirts every weekend. Each night, he set the table for breakfast: coffee cups for his wife and himself; cereal bowls for their oatmeal; spoons; a small platter for donuts or buns; or whatever delight he would purchase in the morning; sugar and creamer. The coffee pot was arranged, ready for morning percolation. I watched him... and was greatly honored when I saw him add another bowl, tea cup and juice glass for me. My parents were both teachers and their schools started hours before mine. My mother dropped me off early before work, so that Grandpapa could drive me to school every morning. Nanabelle was the night owl who stayed up late to watch her favorite shows, so she often came down later than he.

I became a welcome and regular guest to their private morning ritual which happened every morning after Grandpapa returned from Mass and before I left for school. My grandfather was a disciplined man. He would shine his shoes at night: brown or black wing-tipped shoes, to be exact. I got to observe this ritual over the months we lived with my grandparents after we'd sold our home and before the purchase of our new home was final. I always noticed my grandfather seemed deep in thought during this task of shoe-polishing. When I asked him what he was thinking about, he answered, "I am praying to our Blessed Mother. If you ever need anything, ask Mary. She is your Heavenly Mother and will lead you more deeply to Jesus. She'll always lead you on a sure path to Jesus, as His Mother, and as our Heavenly Mother."

It became written on my heart. Through Grandpapa, I learned I can pray anywhere. I learned also to always prepare for tomorrow. Upon reflection, the same man who was our family's Good Shepherd, who had a servant's heart and set tables and cleaned cheerfully, for himself and for his family, reminded me of Christ humbly bending down to untie the straps of his apostles' sandals to wash their feet. My grandfather taught that it is prayerful to serve others with a cheerful heart, to polish one's shoes, invoke Mary and seek her help, asking the Lord to guide our feet for the journey.

Ponder and Pray

- Grandpapa turned meditative tasks into moments of prayer. Which tasks are conducive to prayer for you?

- Did a grandparent or someone in your life teach a lesson to you through their daily example, like Grandpapa's evening and morning disciplines, or through their wise words, such as Grandpapa's lesson on prayer while shining his shoes?

- Have you ever taught a lesson in these ways? Who do you think may have learned by observing you?

- Grandpapa taught that we should always turn to Mary in prayer. The Immaculate Heart of Mary leads directly to the Sacred Heart of her Son, Jesus. One of the best ways to get closer to Jesus's heart is through Mary's heart. Their hearts are so linked that they cannot be separated. Mary will always lead us on a sure path to her Son's Heart. How are you devoted to the Immaculate Heart of Mary?

- Grandpapa was a man of routine in the morning. The discipline of daily Mass was a prayer to start his day. The Morning Offering to the Sacred Heart of Jesus is a beautiful morning prayer discipline. Would you consider praying this as part of your morning prayer? Or do you already do so?

Let us Pray The Fatima Morning Offering

O my God, in union with the Immaculate Heart of Mary (here kiss the Brown Scapular), I offer Thee the Most Precious Body, Blood, Soul and Divinity of Our Lord, Jesus Christ, joining with it my every thought, word and action of this day.

O my Jesus, I desire today to gain every indulgence and merit I can, and I offer them, together with myself, to Mary Immaculate, that she may best apply them to the interests of Thy Most Sacred Heart.

Precious Blood of Jesus, save us!

Immaculate Heart of Mary, pray for us!

Most Sacred Heart of Jesus, have mercy on us!

Amen.

Heart of Jesus, formed by the Holy Ghost in the Womb of the Virgin Mother, have mercy on us.

"Our Lady of Carmel and Saints"
Pietro Novelli

"Salvator Mundi"
Titian

The Lesson of The Wave

"Many people spread their cloaks on the road, and others spread leafy branches that they had cut from the fields. Those preceding him as well as those following kept crying out; 'Hosanna! Blessed is he who comes in the name of the Lord!'"– Mk 11:8-9

"Flevit super illam" (detail)
Enrique Simonet

The Wave

A Beauty that cannot be held— I learned
from you— that there's a certain pain in parting;
in never knowing which goodbye will be
the last. There is a dogwood wound,
a secret pain, beneath a wave—
like the one you'd give each time we'd go—
A wave that says: I don't want you to leave.
I want to be back at your side. Instead,
you forge ahead and sigh a bit inside—
But it's the march of love.

M ake prayer the breakfast of the day," writes poet Francis Etheredge. Grandpapa did that and then some. When my grandfather returned from morning Mass, he'd walk to the corner store and return with an Entenmann's cake. Always in a blue and white box – sometimes cheese danish, other times a blackout cake or coffee crumb buns. He'd share it with me with a cup of tea after our cereal. Sometimes he'd drive to the store for his morning paper and tell me to pick out candy to bring to school. After I would shyly choose one, he would urge me, "Now my dear, how about a Mary Jane? Some candy buttons? A Milky Way?" Now, this was the way to begin the day!

Our drives to school were rich in conversation. We would share our opinions of the houses we passed. One day, we decided we would each pick our favorite house. We laughed when we both picked the same one: a charming, but time-worn white farmhouse with ivy-covered walls, set back from the road and nestled in the trees. It was an unlikely house to be a favorite, but we both sensed evidence of love within it's walls. We were kindred spirits, after all.

I did not like school much back then. Each day I dreaded the parking lot as we'd approach the school. Grandpapa would get out of his car each time and walk me in and stand by my side, and hold my hand until the first bell rang. After I hugged him and walked down the hall to my classroom, I'd look back and see him standing there still, waving at me his special wave. All the other parents or guardians were long gone. The only person I ever knew who seemed to hate goodbyes as much as me was him. He was famous for walking family to their cars and waving as they drove away, and stayed in place waving until the car was out of sight. He had a signature wave: a circular motion to his right hand that was a cross between a papal blessing and a wax-on, wax-off motion *à la* the Karate Kid. It pulled at my heart every time. It was one of the purest ways I ever felt love. That is what Heaven will be like: no more partings.

Ponder and Pray

- What are your goodbyes like? Do you have a certain wave or phrase of parting?

- Do you have any memory of a "beautiful goodbye" or parting?

- Read "Entry into Jerusalem" (Mark 11) and imagine yourself in the crowd. What do you see? What do you do?

Let us pray: Almighty Arms of Jesus, before you, I with all my faith beg you for comfort. In my difficult situation do not forsake me, Good Jesus. Your Almighty Arms will open and close as You desire to give that tranquility that I so desire. (Make your Petitions) O my God, receive that supplication from a wounded heart that is always fighting for me. With your divine power never let me scramble for want of help. Almighty Jesus assist me to find a shelter in Your celestial country forever, Amen.

Heart of Jesus, substantially united to the Word of God, have mercy on us.

"Adoration of the Magi"
Bartolomé Esteban Murillo

The Lesson of The Gifts

"May the favor of the Lord our God be ours. Prosper the work of our hands! Prosper the work of our hands!" –Psalm 90:17

"The Ointment of the Magdalene"
James Tissot

While There is Time to Give

Blossoms are falling from the tree—
but while you're still here and so am I,
Let me love you lavishly.

Gold pollen is falling from the tree—
but while you're still here and so am I,
Let me love you lavishly.

Red leaves are falling from the tree—
but while you're still here and so am I,
Let me love you lavishly.

Snow drops are falling from the tree—
but while you're still here and so am I,
Let me love you lavishly.

I remember with a sigh
the day I learned that you would die
But while you're here and so am I—
Let me love you lavishly.

My mother came into my bedroom and with a look of dread told me about Grandpapa's results from his doctor: he was diagnosed with cancer and had only months to live. I was nine years old. We talked about it together for some time and cried. One of the greatest lessons my mother ever taught me was something she said that night. She told me that Grandpapa would grow weaker and that he might start to look different. She said that even though I was just a child, would see my beloved Grandpapa look differently and it would be hard to see these sorrowful changes, I mustn't ever be afraid of him; and I mustn't let him feel embarrassed. Especially because I was a child, she explained, he would worry for me. He wouldn't want me to be scared, or overwhelmed.

I resolved to heed her words. I would let him see in my face only admiration. That guidance from my mother was a touchstone moment for me, as it would determine the way I would henceforth approach life. And so, when she left the room, I prayed, asking Mary for strength, and Jesus to look over Grandpapa. I wiped the tears away and decided I had to do something – to put the sorrow somewhere, to be of some help.

I noticed a pile of construction paper and crayons on my desk and made a vow, then and there, that I would make a card for Grandpapa every remaining day of his life. My daily cards depicted all of the things he and I did together, always showing him in his signature tie, and always drawing at least one red heart.

My mission was underway immediately. I even tape-recorded, with the help of my dad, my playing some of Grandpapa's favorite piano tunes on the piano so he could listen to them anytime he liked. They included "Clair de Lune" and "I Left My Heart in San Francisco." I now had a more meaningful reason to practice my piano and I learned to love lavishly in those days. I also learned that the gifts given didn't always come in the form I might have expected.

For an example of this, I think back to one day, when Grandpapa's prognosis was growing worse, that my mother and I went over to the Red House to help out. Nanabelle gave my mom a long shopping list of supplies Grandpapa needed from the pharmacy, and as my mother headed out to go get them, I stayed with Nanabelle to keep her company. We had lunch together, and when it was finished, Nanabelle said, "Grandpapa is sleeping, Annabelle. Could you watch him while I go out to the market to get a few things? I won't be long."

I recognized the opportunity I had been given. She needed me, and I could do something for her, and for Grandpapa. This was a real chance to be of help, a concrete way to serve. She rarely had any time alone, when she wasn't at Grandpapa's side; usually someone else ran all the errands for her. I knew she needed a break. I thought of all the responsibility she'd had on her shoulders since she was a young girl, and was glad to be likewise called upon to help my family. I told her she could count on me.

About a half hour after she left, Grandpapa awakened. I went in to see if he needed anything, and he was in terrible pain. His bedsores were aching him and he asked me to bring him pillows, as many as I could. With each pillow I brought, first bed pillows, then couch pillows, he breathed easier, tucking them under his legs and arms to offset the pressure.

Nanabelle came home and found me hurrying around the house, two pillows under my arms. "His bed sores are hurting," I said. "He's asking for all the pillows I can find." She joined me in the hunt, and we found enough to settle him in, comfortably and peacefully. Gradually, he drifted into a nap. She put the kettle on and we sat down at the kitchen table. "Well, I don't know if there's a pillow left in the house that's not in Grandpapa's bed," she remarked with a little chuckle.

"Actually, I even gave him the doll's pillow. He said it was perfect for behind his neck," I said, and that made both of us smile and break the exhaustion and worry with the whimsical thought of even my doll being of assistance.

We had tea and a slice of cake, and then Nanabelle opened up her pocketbook and handed me a glittery pen she'd picked up for me among the curiosities near the counter of the fruit and vegetable market. She'd noticed me admiring it the last time I was there with her. I was delighted to have this shiny pen to write my stories with, and touched that even in the midst of all she had to do, she'd thought of me and brought me a gift.

"You earned it, Annabelle. You were a great help to me today. Thank you for taking such good care of Grandpapa while I got out to the market."

My mother walked in with the parcels just then, and after we'd put them away and got ready to leave, I hugged Nanabelle goodbye and said, "You should prepare yourself. He had a very bad day today. I expect he'll be going to the hospital tonight."

When the call came later, my parents and I raced to the Red House just in time to follow the ambulance to the hospital.

"Annabelle knew," I heard my grandmother say. "I was ready for it; because she knew." She never forgot that story; she reminded me of it for many years after; recounting how she'd been organized and prepared because of my warning, and that as soon as he showed severe signs, she was ready to go. She said it had been a gift to her.

It wasn't a gift I expected to give, any more than the pillows we'd gathered for Grandpapa. But it was really a gift for me, too. It's a privilege to serve those we love, while we can. Thank God for the opportunities He gives us to do just that. Here is the lesson I learned: While people are still with us, let us anoint them, help them, and love them lavishly. Let's not wait until the funerals to shed the tears, and break open the alabaster jars. We think of the sinful woman who cried upon

Jesus' feet, anointed them with perfume and dried them with her hair. Of her Jesus said, "She has done a beautiful thing to me... she did what she could. She poured perfume on my body beforehand to prepare for my burial."(Mk 14:6-8)

As the Magi traveled from afar to bring priceless gifts to the Christ child, let us lavishly care for those we love and give gifts as though they are pearls of great price. So let us send the flowers; give the effusive compliment; serve a meal on the good china; wash the dishes and gather the pillows: now. Let us take the time. Let us not put off until tomorrow what we can do for God today.

Ponder and Pray

- Making cards was a healing act benefiting the giver and the receiver in this lesson. How have you dealt positively in difficult times?

- When a loved one is suffering, what is the work of your hands?

- How do you, or how do you wish to, love lavishly?

- What gifts are you known for that you bring to family or friends at special times? Is there a regular contribution you give, such as bringing dessert, making a special dish, cleaning up at the party, knitting scarves, or making crafts, etc.?

Let us Pray The Holy Heart of Jesus Prayer: O most holy Heart of Jesus, fountain of every blessing, I adore You, I love You, and with a lively sorrow for my sins, I offer You this poor heart of mine. Make me humble, patient, pure, and wholly obedient to Your will. Grant, good Jesus, that I may live in You and for You. Protect me in the midst of danger; comfort me in my afflictions. Give me health of body, assistance in my temporal needs, Your blessing on all that I do, and the grace of a holy death.

Amen.

Heart of Jesus, of Infinite Majesty, have mercy on us.

Window detail, All Saints Catholic Church
St. Peters, Missouri

"Man of Sorrows"
William Dyce

The Lesson of The Garbage

"Hear my words, O Lord; listen to my sighing. Hear my cry for help, my King, my God!" –Psalm 5:2-3

"Starry Night Over the Rhone"
Vincent van Gogh

Take the Time

Along the way, take time to smell the flowers—
a sign said in the hallway of the stairs
of my grandmother's house.
So every morning, when she would wake
and journey down to breakfast,
she was reminded of the holy pause—
that comes with noticing the beauty unexpected—
even in the busyness of things.

And so, even while care-giving, her rounds
of cleaning, cooking, gathering the trash
accumulated from his medicines,
boxes of tissues, cans of supplements—
the pilgrim badges of a sacrifice,
both hers and his— his offering up the cross of pain,
her carrying the wooden beam of it in turns—

When she'd emerge from the house where he slept,
to carry bags of trash out to the road—
whether on nights of crickets or of snow,
she'd lift her neck and search the sky for stars,
a breath of heaven's garden in the sky—
Ephphatha, Be opened— while deaf and mute
with tiredness and dread, she'd watch the moon
sigh with the constellations, take the time.

Nanabelle was not a tall or sturdily-built woman. She was petite in structure but her spirit was mighty. She was always in motion; there was always a twinkle in her eye and her mind crackled with ideas. She was not an extraverted personality by nature – but no one would ever guess this because she loved people and everyone was always so happy being around her. She had opinions aplenty, but she was a kind listener. I have a feeling she learned a great deal watching her own mother who raised ten children.

When Grandpapa became sick, Nanabelle carried her cross, caring for him lovingly and patiently. There are two words in Greek for body, *sarx* and *soma*. While the *soma* is the idealized body, that of a healthy athlete or beauty, the *sarx* is the sweat, the blood, the vulnerably broken body. In the Greek translation, Jesus says "This is my *sarx* which will be given up for you." Nanabelle cared for Grandpapa's *sarx*, and in so doing, she cared for Christ, serving him in His pain. She never complained about the work it entailed. Grandpapa also never once complained. Instead, he worried about her. Their love for each other was so evident and the sorrow they bore bravely was a testament of their faith and fortitude.

During this time, which lasted nine months, Nana had not stopped "being there" for her family; and we all did what we could to be of help to her. But she bore the brunt of the burden and drew upon her faith in God with an indomitable spirit one day at a time.

She told us that one healing ritual that happened quite by accident was, as she brought the garbage out each night to place in the larger outside pails, she would pause and look to the stars and breathe in the cool air and pray. "One windy night the tissues from the pail blew wildly down the street in the dark like tumbleweeds," she told us with a chuckle. I am convinced she would offer these stories to us to give us a compass for our own lives. I hung on her every word.

I learned from her that perseverance, humor, and seeking God's beauty are valuable companions in hard times and I learned tenacity in prayer looking up at the heavens. She found beauty in the midst of garbage, and soma in the midst of sarx. The Creator's magnificent handiwork eased the pain of my family's *Via Dolorosa*.

Ponder and Pray

- As Nanabelle put out the garbage each night, she looked up at the stars and prayed. When did you pray during an unlikely time?

- Do you know a friend or family member who showed courage as a caregiver of a loved one? Was it you?

- Nanabelle found humor as she watched the tissues blowing "like tumbleweeds in the wind." When has humor broken the spell of a sad or lonely time in your life?

Let us pray: Sacred Heart of Jesus, today I wish to live in You, in Your Grace, in which I desire at all costs to persevere. Keep me from sin and strengthen my will by helping me to keep watch over my senses, my imagination, and my heart. Help me to correct my faults which are the source of sin. I beg You to do this, O Jesus, through Mary, Your Immaculate Mother.

Amen.

Heart of Jesus, Holy Temple of God, have mercy on us.

"Starry Night"
Vincent van Gogh

"Entry Into Jerusalem"
Pietro Lorenzetti

The Lesson of
The Palms

"and now he was approaching the slope of the Mount of Olives, the whole multitude of his disciples began to praise God aloud with joy for all the mighty deeds they had seen. They proclaimed: 'Blessed is the King who comes in the name of the Lord. Peace in heaven and glory in the highest!'" –Lk 19:37-38

"Christ Entering Jerusalem"
Jean-Hippolyte Flandrin

The Palms

When Jesus rode into Jerusalem
for the last time, green fronds were held aloft—
to greet Him like a king.
That is the day you died. Palm Sunday, yes—
and why? It taught the ones you left behind
that holding Love so sacred as you did
led to the kind of wave—
embracing the welcome of God—
the Beauty that forever can be held.

My Grandpapa drew on Scripture and prayer during this time. My Grandmother asked him one day, "How are you able to undergo radiation each time so bravely?" His answer was brief, as he was walking to his treatment, "Isaiah." So the secret was out... He found courage from the Book of the Prophet Isaiah. All his adult children, when they got home that day, went directly to their Bible and explored Isaiah more deeply. This is a memory they often share. They needed courage, too.

It was the Lenten season – a solemn, holy time in our Catholic faith – when we journey with Christ to his Crucifixion and death on Calvary. The family was simultaneously on a journey of sorrow with our beloved Grandpapa as he journeyed to the Father, and to Calvary, the hospital for terminal patients. He wished to go there as a final retreat of sorts. The time had come. Grandpapa rode in the back of the ambulette, facing out the back window, with his oldest son "riding shotgun," as they both put it. Nanabelle and the others followed in a caravan of cars, and Grandpapa gave his signature wave to all. When they arrived at Calvary, he smiled and gave everyone a "thumbs-up." It is a unique place, this Calvary – like its namesake, it brought a rare sense of peace and joy amidst pain and fear. He knew where he must be and he chose wisely.

Propped up in his bed he was dressed all in pure white with the faded marks of his wounds; a light pink in the bandages, like a dogwood blossom. There was a crucifix overhead. This was a Lenten journey all his family would oddly cherish. They witnessed faith in his living and dying. He was not a perfect man – but as his wife said many times, "he was not an empty suit. He did his work." During his end days, he wrote on paper to them, *When I see Jesus I'm going to bow.* The man who stood at my side and held my hand, who waved faithfully until all were out of sight, left us on the day our faith sets aside for waving – waving to the Lord as he entered Jerusalem for greeting Jesus with jubilant palms. That Palm Sunday, as my grandfather entered through Heaven's gates and bowed, there was everywhere a great and faithful waving.

The material things he left behind: a watch, a pair of glasses, a Cross pen, a comb, and a brown accordion file-folder of every card I ever made him.

Ponder and Pray

Grandpapa found courage and comfort in the words of Isaiah. And how beautiful was his faith to seek refuge in Scripture!

- Do you have a Scripture passage that comforts you, or several?

- What Scripture passage challenges you the most? Share, or journal.

Let us pray: The Family Prayer to the Sacred Heart:

Sacred Heart of Jesus, we entrust our family to You. Look down upon us and reveal to us the treasures of love, goodness, and grace in Your Heart. Forgive our sins and fortify our weakness, that we may serve You faithfully as You deserve. These favors we ask for ourselves and for every family in our neighborhood and homeland. Heart of Jesus, pierced by a soldier's lance on Calvary, be our refuge in life and our gateway to Paradise.

Amen.

Heart of Jesus, Tabernacle of the Most High, have mercy on us.

"Entry of Christ into Jerusalem"
Anthony van Dyck

"Return of the Prodigal Son"
Rembrandt van Rijn

The Lesson of The Bow

"The LORD is my strength and song." –Ex 15:2

"Come, let us bow down and worship." –Psalm 95:6

"The Healing of the Ten Lepers"
James Tissot

The Song of the Tenth Leper

My grandfather told us when he'd meet the Lord
he'd bow. Before God's greatness, overwhelmed
with awe and wonder, he knew words would fail.
When love wins over power and your pride,
you bow. The very knees of your heart fold.
Each one of us is called to be the one,
the one leper of ten who praises God,
falls on our face at His feet and
gives thanks for salvation, life and love.
How can we stand before such beauty?
How can we not sink down, like a child,
look up with trust and gratitude and sing
of Creator's majesty and our Savior's sacrifice.
What an act of the will: to will to serve.
Praise be to God for giving us the chance
to choose to love, to choose to serve,
to know that bowing is the only thing
when in the presence of a king.
It is a grace, a gift, relief
to curve our body down, like a tall reed
lowering its fronds along the sand
in the presence of the tide
and, in so doing,
feel the power of the sea.

Nanabelle gave my father an important assignment. Grandpapa had requested the Kate Smith version of the hymn, "How Great Thou Art" to be played at his funeral. She put my dad on the case to find this bygone treasure. It was not easy. This was before internet search engines and the hunt was on. The words of that hymn are filled with references which spoke to my grandfather's soul like seeing God in nature, calling us to the mystery of the sufferings of Christ, and of course the powerful words, "Then I will bow in humble adoration and there proclaim 'My God how great Thou art!'" My dad found the tape. Everyone in the family was doing their share to tribute the family's shepherd. It was a kind of healing for each to have tasks to fulfill, lest all crumble under the sorrow.

At the end of the funeral Mass, after Communion, and just before leaving the church together, my father reverently stood, bowed to the main altar, walked to the side altar, and knelt down to the portable stereo, hitting "play." The soulful sounds of "How Great Thou Art" echoed throughout the church and into everyone's hearts. As my father bowed and knelt to start the music, Kate Smith sang of the bow that Grandpapa had planned.

Ponder and Pray

- What do you want to say and/or do when you see Jesus?
- Do you have a favorite hymn that inspires you in your faith, as "How Great Thou Art" inspired Grandpapa?
- Why do you like it? Any particular lyric touch you?

• Have you had an experience where bowing or kneeling has enhanced your prayer?

Let us pray: From the depth of my nothingness, I prostrate myself before Thee, O Most Sacred, Divine and Adorable Heart of Jesus, to pay Thee all the homage of love, praise and adoration in my power. Amen. - St. Margaret Mary Alacoque

Heart of Jesus, House of God and Gate of Heaven, have mercy on us.

"Moses and Joshua in the Tabernacle"
James Tissot

"The Incredulity of Saint Thomas"
François-Joseph Navez

The Lesson of
The Paperweight

"Then he said to Thomas, put your finger here and see my hands, and bring your hand and put it into my side, and do not be unbelieving, but believe." –Jn 20:27

"The Lord gave and the Lord has taken away. Blessed be the name of the Lord." –Job 1:21

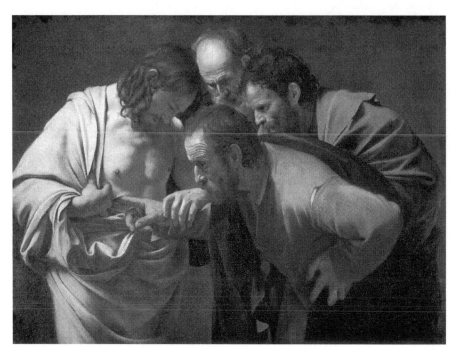

"The Incredulity of Saint Thomas"
Caravaggio

The Weight of Resurrection

The paperweight might have been left behind.
Instead, when it rolled off a flatbed,
my father pulled over for a closer look—
saving what others had passed.

Holding the blown-glass globe
he smoothed away the dirt and gravel,
and felt its blemished texture
perfect when created, rough from the fall.

The maker's breath and crucible's fire
had formed the glass dome
which held a flower within—
golden petals, arched tendrils.

The damaged weight held a bright Resurrection —
that my father carried home.
He gave it to the child I was,
not knowing he would soon die.

As he placed it in my hand,
his thumb filled the gash
where the glass had crashed,
but hadn't shattered.

I asked: with such a deep wound,
why didn't it break?
He said: It's stronger now.
It's like the soul.

He took my hand through a sunset field,
not knowing the flower under glass
soon would collect dust on my shelf
as he lingered three weeks in a coma—

Our House of the Sacred Heart

And after his death—
I took up his bruised prize,
cupped the familiar brokenness in my hands,
and pressed my finger into the gouge—

As Thomas did
when he touched the wound
that brought him home.

"The Doubting Thomas"
Leendert van der Cooghen

My parents liked to say I was a "born poet," and they were perceptive enough to notice this in me, and nourish my gift. Words were my first love and I delighted in trying to use interesting words even when I was very young. My mother tells the story of me, sniffling and sulking at two years old, declaring, "I'm miz-able!" My father liked to tell a story that when I was three, I told him, very dramatically, "Daddy, I love you so much, my heart is unruly." Fortunately for me, our house was filled with books. My father was an English teacher and professor of Speech. My mother, also a school teacher, would take walks with me and we'd play games of not only finding shapes in the clouds but also trying to come up with similes and metaphors for them. I was an avid reader and writer by about age five. My father was my editor. I would value his honest opinions of my work and knew if he was trying to be too kind or if he genuinely admired what I'd written. I loved the look on his face when he really liked it. I loved climbing those stairs to his wonderful office.

I pored over my Children's Illustrated Bible long into the night when I should have turned out my light. I made a connection that climbing the stairs to my father's office was like ascending Jacob's Ladder. The climb was symbolic – he was a tower of wisdom to me. He would be reading, or writing lesson plans, often underlining the texts he'd teach his students the next day, and making notes in the margins on insights he could bring them. One insight he brought me was through his regular declaration to me, "You are a forest with one tree." I understood this poetic proclamation from him better as the years passed. What an eloquent way to explain a child to herself: a seeming contradiction in terms, one person containing multitudes of depth, one tree holding a forest within. This parable of the one-treed forest planted a seed I would tend throughout my life. My father gave the most unusual kind of gifts, and they always appealed to the born poet in me.

My dad liked to find unexpected treasures whether a rare coin or stamp, or wildflowers on the side of a country road for my mom, or even a brass elevator button bearing the number 7 that he found in an elevator on my seventh birthday and brought me with a triumphant grin.

A few months after my grandfather's passing, my Dad came home from work and his eyes shone as he handed me a surprise he found. He said he'd been driving when something bounced out of a truck in front of him and rolled to the side of the road. It was a beautiful blown-glass paperweight with a yellow lily inside it. There was a gouge where the paperweight had fallen, but not broken. He pulled his car over to investigate and when he saw the beautiful weight still intact despite its wound, he took it home. He was smiling broadly as he handed it to me, and said, "It's like the good soul." The soul can be made even more beautiful through the difficult times we face.

As I placed my thumb against the jagged gash, I was reminded of the wounds of Jesus and the redeeming beauty that came from them. I felt that my broken heart, missing Grandpapa, was something Jesus understood. It was something my father also understood. I realized he, too, was hurting and found comfort in finding and giving this gift. My father was a good and wise father and teacher. What a beautiful and simple way this was to bring healing to his child in mourning.

Ponder and Pray

- Do you possess a keepsake from a loved one? What story does it tell?

- How might you explain the existence of the soul to a child?

Let us pray The Act of Love to the Sacred Heart

How great, O my Jesus, is the extent of Thine excessive charity! Thou hast prepared for me, of Thy most precious Body and Blood, a divine banquet, where Thou givest me Thyself without reserve. What hath urged Thee to this excess of love? Nothing but Thine own most loving Heart.

O adorable Heart of my Jesus, furnace of Divine Love, receive my soul into the wound of Thy most Sacred Passion, that in this school of charity I may learn to make a return of love to that God Who hast given me such wonderful proofs of His love.

Heart of Jesus, burning furnace of Charity, have mercy on us.

"Jacob's Ladder"
William Blake

"Praying Hands"
Albrecht Dürer

The Lesson of The Hands

"I will not forget you. I have held you in the palm of my hand." –Isa 49:15

"The Virgin and Child"
Sandro Botticelli

Mary Recalls the Prophecy of Simeon

A mother knows her son's hands like her own.
She studies them from birth—each fingernail
is halo-shaped. Soft skin over strong bone,
each line and dimple forms a sacred braille.
While Simeon foretold, I held Christ's hand.
And that was when the blade first pierced my soul.
I knew that to redeem a broken land,
my child's palms could not remain smooth, whole.
The earth is punctured, seeded, before sprouts
grow forth. Then fruit is gathered, branches pruned.
There must be something for the soul who doubts
to press their fingers into, like a wound.
The piercing of my soul provides a sieve—
for sifting death from those who long to live.

For sifting death from those who long to live,
the piercing of my soul provides a sieve—
to press their fingers into, like a wound.
There must be something for the soul who doubts.
Grow forth! Then fruit is gathered, branches pruned.
The earth is punctured, seeded, before sprouts.
My child's palms could not remain smooth, whole.
I knew that— to redeem a broken land...
And that was when the blade first pierced my soul.
While Simeon foretold, I held Christ's hand.
Each line and dimple formed a sacred braille,
was halo-shaped. Soft skin over strong bone,
I'd studied them from birth—each fingernail.
A mother knows her son's hands like her own.

Just months after my father had given me the paperweight holding the golden lily, and spoken of the bruised, yet beautiful soul, he suddenly and tragically was rushed to the hospital in critical condition.

I asked to ride with with my father in the ambulance. When I say I asked, I really mean I insisted, stubbornly. My mother and I got in the ambulance, and each of us took one of his hands. My father was still holding on to consciousness, though he could not speak. I remember studying his hands so I could memorize the feel of them, the palm and fingers. And in the last litany I spoke to him, I repeated the words, "I love you," again and again as the screaming ambulance sped its way to the hospital. It was the only thing I wanted to say. In that space, it was all that mattered. I kissed his strong hand, pressed it to my cheek, held it in my hands. It never occurred to me that I was being repetitive or that one "I love you" was enough. I wanted to fill a lifetime of "I love you"s into his heart while I knew he could still hear me.

Little did I know that this moment would serve as a strong inspiration, many years later, as I wrote a book about the Rosary, entitled *Sacred Braille*, emphasizing the tactile quality of the Rosary and likening the decades of beads to fingers on the hand of a beloved parent.

Each bead in a decade becomes one of Mary's beautiful fingers... fingers that cared for Jesus when he was a child, fingers that touched him as he died. Each bead in a decade becomes a way to clasp the hands of Jesus into your own... the hands so extremely pained with their wounds of love. Each bead in a decade is a way to thank him, to touch his strong and sacrificing fingers. The "Hail Marys" and "Our Fathers" are prayerful "I love you"s.

The Hands

May we use the mouths and hands we are given on this side of Heaven to tell the Immaculate and Sacred Hearts of our love, while there's still time. Let's do it every day, no matter how tired we are, or busy. Why? It is a way to bind our hands, our lives, to Heaven. And so let us not put off until tomorrow what we can do for God today. As we pray the Rosary, let us hold the beads or if we don't have beads, our own fingers, with as much closeness as though it is the hand of the person we have loved and lost... and rejoice that we will never lose Mary or Jesus, if we keep reaching for their hands through those beads.

Putting this into practice: while on an overnight retreat some years back, I slept in a little room with an old crucifix, and noticed the left hand was missing, had somehow broken off. A couple of years after that, I read the story of the Infant of Prague, a statue of the child Jesus that had been discarded during war and its hands broken off. A story goes that as a priest named Fr. Cyril prayed before this statue in 1637, a voice spoke to him and said:

> Have mercy on Me and I will have mercy on you.
> Give Me hands and I will give you peace.
> The more you honor Me, the more I will bless you.

I asked the retreat center to give me permission to return and find the room with the broken crucifix, and to remove it and try to have it repaired. They allowed me to keep it as long as I'd like. One artist I found tried and then said it was too hard a job for him, and other artists admitted outright that it was too tough to fix. I am still seeking a way to repair the hand, but for now it is a daily reminder that, to quote St. Teresa of Avila, "Christ has no body now but yours. No hands, no feet on earth but yours. Yours are the eyes through which he looks compassion on this world. Yours are the feet with which he walks to do good. Yours are the hands through which he blesses all the world."

And so, unto our last breath, may we hold hands with God's mysteries. May we be that hand of blessing in every way we can find. We know what it's like to lose someone we love, to hold the hand of someone one day and not the next. May we magnify that lesson in Christ and make our hands serve and hold fast to the Rosary, to the goal of being Christ's hands, and to the memory of the last time we held the hand of someone we love.

In the meantime, the crucifix with the broken hand is a constant visual reminder to me, and to my family, of the daily obligation to ask for the graces necessary to be the hand of Christ; to serve, to make prayerful reparation; to fill the wounds of Christ with our love, and repeatedly offer our love to the Sacred Heart of Jesus.

Ponder and Pray

- How have you been Christ's hands?
- Does this lesson validate your love of the Rosary, or inspire you to pray the Rosary more regularly?
- Write or find a short prayer asking the Sacred Heart to guide the work of your hands each day.

Let us pray the Prayer to Honor the Miraculous Infant Jesus of Prague

Divine Infant Jesus, I want to give You my hands today. I want to serve You with all my heart and make You known and loved. Doing Your will is the source of my inner peace and joy.

Divine Infant, I give You my hands to touch those I meet with Your love and peace. I ask You to heal those in pain, to encourage the hopeless, to console the sorrowing, and to provide for those in want. I ask You to reach out to the lonely. I especially plead for the many people suffering from great poverty and injustice.

Miraculous Infant, I believe that You love me and know all of my needs. I place them in Your hands, especially my present concerns (mention here). I trust in Your love and care. I want to honor and praise You, now and forever.

Amen.

Heart of Jesus, abode of Justice and Love, have mercy on us.

"The Flight into Egypt"
George Hitchcock

The Lesson of The Queen Anne's Lace

"As one whom his mother comforts, so I will comfort you; you shall be comforted in Jerusalem." –Isa 66:13

"And his mother treasured up all these things in her heart." –Lk 2:51

"Mother and Daughter on a Swing (Happy Times)"
Robert Walker Mac Beth

Queen Anne's Lace

for my mother

Once, at Benner's Farm in mid-morning—
I stood before a long tire swing that swept the fields.
The child I was would not ride the wind alone.
So you leapt on with me—and we flung ourselves forward.

With fingers full of rope we pitched towards the clouds—
and when we landed, you took my hand.
We who had journeyed the air walked through wildflowers.
You gave me an armful of Queen Anne's Lace, stems anointed
in dust.

How could we have known what we would travel together?
How could we have known what we would travel together?
I only knew it was because of you that I had jumped and
landed—
and the wild bouquet you offered was a benediction.

You see what others miss—
and taught me to love the bloom of a wild carrot
like a cultivated rose. When I see it lining roads and meadows,
I see you, making beauty from my stray threads.

These days, over my piano, a print by George Hitchcock: The
Flight into Egypt.
Mary presses her child close as they navigate a field of Queen
Anne's Lace.
She looks down at the white aerial filigree—
rooted to earth, draped in cobweb.

They ground her beauty as she journeys her unknown field.
What Mary imagines as she presses forward—
The way Saint Anne, her mother, would enfold her,
with arms like wings.

D uring the painful days of my father's travail and death, my mother was my greatest source of consolation. Those many times she would hold me, in our shared grief, I would be flooded with memories of a sunny day we had shared when I was very little. It was a day that stood out to me as emblematic of our close bond, and her guiding force of strength, joy, and her consistently wise and loving example. I once read a quote by Abraham Lincoln: "Everything I am or hope to be, I owe to my angel mother," and I feel the same way. I could confide anything safely in her, and she made my faith come more deeply alive. She was my constant supporter, and was an earthly model to me of the heavenly love of our Blessed Mother.

In the Living Room of the House of the Sacred Heart, over the upright piano, was a print of George Hitchcock's *The Flight into Egypt*. In the image, Mary holds Baby Jesus close to her heart as she sits atop the donkey, and St. Joseph walks behind, scanning for danger and ensuring that he literally "has their back." In the foreground is a field of wildflowers.

When the nursery school planned an autumn outing for the four-year-olds in their charge, my mom decided to be a "trip mom" and came along on the bus to Benner's Farm. It was a brisk, sunny morning as we headed out, hand-in-hand to walk among the fields and see the sights. One memory lingers of that day that so well explains the relationship I have with my mother. We walked the trails to the pumpkin patch which then led us to climb a hill overlooking the fields. Atop the hill was a tire swing attached to a zip line inviting the children to ride for a spell, flying down the hill, around a corner, across an acre of farmland, and land on the other side. My mom recognized my hesitancy. I didn't want to ride alone and out of sight. So with an impish grin, she jumped on behind me and together we swooped forward. Our heads thrown back in laughter, we flew through the air across the landscape. The sun was warm, and I felt her arms around me as we gazed at the bold orange pumpkins below us and a vivid blue sky above us, and the breeze embracing us. When we landed, we found ourselves thick in a field of wildflowers and Queen Anne's Lace. It was as though we had stepped inside that George Hitchcock painting above my grandmother's piano.

"I've always loved Queen Anne's lace," my mother told me as she picked me a big bouquet of the lacy blooms. She was more excited about these wildflowers than I'd seen her get over a bouquet of orchids.

My Grandpapa told my mother when she was young, "Your name honors Mary's mother. It means 'Beautiful St. Anne.'" I wonder what Blessed Mother Mary saw her mother do, heard her mother say, that would prepare her for the many trials *she* would face.

Ponder and Pray

- Among your childhood memories, what event highlights a trait you or a loved one possess, such as courage, joy, or wisdom?

- Like the swing ride of mother and daughter in the lesson, what event in your past may have been pointing to something you were perhaps being prepared for in your future?

- Just for fun, do you have a favorite flower? What is it about the flower that makes it special?

- When you think of St. Anne with her daughter, our Blessed Mother, what do you imagine? Can you picture Mary, held as a baby in St. Anne's arms? Can you picture St. Anne teaching Mary when she was a little girl? What prayer rises in you as you imagine our Blessed Mother's relationship with her mother?

Let us pray The Daily Prayer to the Sacred Heart

Sacred Heart of our Saviour, please bless us as the new day dawns. May we grow today in Your friendship, in helpfulness to others, in gratitude for Your benefits beyond number. May Christly love fill our hearts, guard our thoughts, and inspire our actions. Jesus, we believe in Your love for us. We trust in You and want to remain forever in the safe haven of Your loving Heart.

Amen.

Heart of Jesus, full of Goodness and Love, have mercy on us.

"Saint Anne Teaching the Virgin to Read"
Bartolomé Esteban Murillo

"Winter Landscape with Church"
Caspar David Friedrich

The Lesson of The Magnolias

Exhortation to the Night Watch to Bless God

"O come, Bless the Lord, all you servants of the Lord, you who stand in the house of the Lord throughout the nights!" –Psalm 134:1

"Giant Magnolias On A Blue Velvet Cloth"
Martin Johnson Heade

Magnolia in Midwinter

For Nanabelle on her 95th Birthday

The gardener of winter
has given you a rose.
There is a grandmother who sings to you
a lullaby, in shades of blue—
as gentle as a springtime bird.
She rocks you in her tree-branch arms.
When you awaken, she pats your head
and refuses to stay in the rocker.
She is time honored-energy,
this wild muse—
a magnolia blooming in midwinter—
through visions scarred and snow-blind.
With laughing gold-brown eyes,
the wild muse speaks to you
in warm breath that touches cold air
clouding your glare—
shaking your stare.
Her voice, when she speaks, is visible.

During a time of profound liminality, while my father lay in a coma, my mother and I clung to each other. Every day brought the looming reality of impending doom. We guarded each other, frightfully aware of the fragility of life. Actually, we both agreed that our strength came from each other and... the other Annabelle in our life, my grandmother, Nanabelle. She completed our trinity. She was our pearl of great price. This was never more clear to me than the time we braved a snow squall together. One day, after teaching, my mom picked me up from school, we stopped to get Nanabelle, and together we all went to sit and pray by my father's bedside. After a long vigil, we left the hospital, as it was getting dark and the weather looked threatening.

The car ride home was very quiet. We thought our own thoughts and I'm sure, inwardly spoke to God. The car was not sounding good – it seemed to be hesitating as my mom accelerated. We were about three-quarters of a mile from Nanabelle's Red House when my mother pulled the car to the side of the road just before the engine stopped. This was before the advent of the cellular phone. We just left the car there and walked to the butcher nearby for dinner meats, then went back to the car for our things, and hatched a plan to walk across the busy turnpike and down a neighborhood street to our refuge, Nanabelle's house. It began to snow. It came down rapidly and wind began to stir up the large, white flakes.

"We can do this! It's not quite a mile from here! There's barely any traffic in all this weather! Let's get home and eat and we'll worry about the car tomorrow!" Nanabelle shouted encouragingly above the snow.

We linked arms together, the three of us, my grandmother in the middle, and slipped and slid across what was normally one of the busiest streets on Long Island, but due to the snow, a ghost town of white. Nanabelle gripped the pork chops and we gripped Nanabelle. We could barely see in all that blinding blur and none of us had gloves. "The three Annabelle's... causin' trouble!" My grandmother giggled. At once, we couldn't stop laughing, an unfamiliar sound in those days of worry and sorrow. Snow blew into our faces as we scurried across to the other side and found our way to Nanabelle's street. "Yeah; we're something else! You know what we are? We're the three Steel Magnolias!" My mom shouted above the wind, summoning images of the recent movie by that title: tales of grit and grace shared between bonded women. We marched together, eyes squinted, heads down, hoods up and over our heads as we watched our weary feet keep pace with each other. "The Steel Magnolias!" I cried out with a laugh. Now all three had declared it. It was official.

The bracing cold stung our faces, the frost laced our hair as we marched, now facing into the storm, arms linked. We'd been shaken from the numbness of grief into a snow globe of a beautiful travail we would conquer together.

As we saw the Red House in the distance, like a heart with a flame of light in the tapestry of white around us, we planned to get washed up and make dinner so we could get our needed rest by retiring early. We arrived in Nana's kitchen, removing our coats, shaking off the snow and unwrapping the food. We moved in harmony, as in a dance. I noticed how we each chose a task that complemented the efforts of another.

I rejoiced aloud, "I am so proud to be an Annabelle!" and we all agreed. We all had bright red cheeks, socks resting perched atop a hot radiator, and an appetite, as the smell of frying pork and sauerkraut filled the room. We ate with abandon, despite our sorrow. This was just one example of the many adventures we three shared. The lesson I learned on this day in my life was not to cower in sorrow and fear, but to push through until you find life and love on the other side. The bracing cold of the snow will pass, and there will be laughter again.

These days, above my living room sofa: a print of three magnolias, white as snow: one in full bloom, one partially opened, and one still a bud. It is a constant reminder of what we faced together, as grandmother, mother and child, and how we three forged ahead anyway — thanks be to God.

Ponder and Pray

- When did you show grace under pressure?
- Did you ever push through grief to find joy on the other side?
- Who is the wild muse (inspiration) of your heart? If you cannot think of a person you have known, then what saint has occupied that role for you? If you don't have this kind of hero, search for one.

Let us pray

May the Sacred Heart of Jesus be adored, glorified, loved and preserved throughout the world now and forever. Sacred Heart of Jesus, pray for us. St.Jude, worker of miracles, pray for us. St Jude, help of the hopeless, pray for us

(Say this prayer 9 times a day for 9 days as a novena)

Heart of Jesus, abyss of all virtues, have mercy on us.

"Allegory of Vanity"
Antonio de Pereda

The Lesson of The Clocks

"Before the Feast of Passover, Jesus knew that his hour had come to pass from this world to the Father. He loved his own in the world and he loved them to the end." –Jn 13:1

"Divine Mercy"
Eugeniusz Kazimirowski

The Persistence of Memory

Our house clocks stopped the day my father died—
at three, the very hour that he passed.
No catch of shifting gears, no pulse defied
his absence. Time itself mourned him. The past
and future froze in one long pause. We kept
this lack of measured music, mourning him—
the clock-lover and watch-buyer. Except,
time offered itself up in grief. The trim
minutes and hours my young father filled,
stopped at the hour of mercy, holding him.
And days after his death, a parcel thrilled
when it arrived. He had ordered a slim,
black-banded watch. On its face, a Dali
painting of melting time. His memory.

One summer night in childhood I ran
chasing a firefly. Then I let go.
That is the way my father died; the man
felt time dripping off of his fingers: slow,
honey-paced drizzle. But he shook it free
when he beheld a distant speck of light,
and lunged, then with a laugh, fell forward. He
rejected past and future for the bright
and promised steadfastness of the long now.
My father's unworn watch bore on its face,
between the marks of twelve and six, the brow
of melting time. The hour of mercy's grace
would mark my father's countenance, though age
had not. He had not reached the fading stage.

It was only nine months after we lost Grandpapa that my dear father died. He suffered an aneurysm, was in a coma for weeks, and succumbed. There was no time for card-making, no musical tapes of piano-playing to be made, no talks with my mom about what was to come, and how we might better cope. It was so sudden. There was no warning. Each day of the vigil we were gripped in fear and sorrow.

At the Emergency Room, miraculously, all the family arrived in ones and twos, hearts and hands ready and willing to take on our pain. My grandmother was there to ease another burden, and as the evening labored on to early morning, she took me to the Red House of the Sacred Heart to rest. I told her I couldn't eat a thing, and I didn't think it would have been possible, until she gave me a cup of malted milk and I drank it all.

My father died at three o'clock, on a Friday, the day of the week devoted to the Passion of Jesus, Divine Mercy, and the Sacred Heart of Jesus. When my mom and I returned to our home to gather some things to take back to the Red House, we saw that all the clocks had stopped at three o'clock. It was as if the house knew its dome was absent. Three o'clock, the hour marking the end of a teacher's school day; three o'clock, the hour marking Christ's death on Good Friday; three o'clock, the Hour of Divine Mercy. For the sake of his sorrowful Passion...

I knew that soon there would not be a way I could give my dad, on this side of Heaven, concrete acts of love. I wanted to serve while I could. I wanted to make my father proud and so I welcomed each mourner as they entered the funeral home. I thanked each one for coming and listened as they told me of their love and admiration for my father. His students said he spoke of me often. He told stories of our many adventures together. They told me he was proud of me.

At my request, I read the second reading at his funeral Mass. It was from 2 Timothy 4:6-8: "I have fought the good fight... I have finished the race..." I liked this reading. My father was a marathon runner and so it comforted me. My legs trembled as I stood and read, my stomach sank, but I read clearly and unwaveringly. No amount of courage could dull the piercing pain of living through one of my own life's sorrowful mysteries. But when I was finished, I gazed for a moment at the stained glass of Christ the triumphant King. The hardship of standing to read on the worst day of my life was my offering to both my fathers, earthly and heavenly.

My father's teaching days were done... or so I'd thought. The clocks in my house had stopped at three o'clock. I hadn't been able to speak to my father in his last days. We had only been able to pray for him and not with him. But the Lord gave even as He took away; giving my father the day of the week and the hour of His own death to comfort us all. My father ended every work week as a teacher at three o'clock on a Friday and his life as a teacher culminated, by the grace of God, in an unforgettable lesson spotlighting God's mercy even in the face of unthinkable pain.

Ponder and Pray

- This lesson describes that the clocks in the house were all stopped at 3:00 pm, the Hour of Divine Mercy. This brought comfort to the family. The Chaplet of Divine Mercy is a very meaningful afternoon discipline. Has this chaplet played an important role in your life? If you don't already, would you consider praying this as part of your daily routine?

- Part of the Divine Mercy devotion is praying the short aspiration, "Jesus, I trust in You!" Even if the one praying has a hard time with trust, simply saying this prayer with faith, hope, and love, especially in times of anxiety, will increase our trust and decrease our worries. How is your prayer life with regard to trust? Would you consider adding this prayer?

- Was there an event in your life that you remember the time at which it happened? For example, did it occur on the feast day of a particular saint, or an important day in our church's liturgical calendar? Perhaps you might research this. Does this information make this event more memorable? How?

- Friday is the day of the week devoted not only to the Passion and Divine Mercy, but also the Sacred Heart of Jesus. All Fridays, not just the ones in Lent, are meant to be days of some penance and sacrifice to better remember the sufferings of Christ. How do you remember this sacrifice at the end of your week? Do you give up meat on Fridays? Have you ever done the "First Friday" devotion, going to Mass and making reparation to the Sacred Heart for nine months in a row? Have you ever sought out time in prayer before the Blessed Sacrament on a Friday? What could you do on a Friday each week to better align yourself to the Passion of Our Lord? How does recalling His Passion make your Friday more meaningful?

Let us Pray the Closing Prayer of the Chaplet of Divine Mercy

Eternal God, in whom mercy is endless and the treasury of compassion — inexhaustible, look kindly upon us and increase Your mercy in us, that in difficult moments we might not despair nor become despondent, but with great confidence submit ourselves to Your holy will, which is Love and Mercy itself.

Heart of Jesus, most worthy of all praise, have mercy on us.

"The Light of the World"
William Holman Hunt

The Lesson of The Door

"I am the door. By me, if any man enter in, he shall be saved: and he shall go in, and go out, and shall find pastures." –Jn 10:9

"Behold, I stand at the door and knock; if any man hear My voice, and open the door, I will come in to him, and will sup with him, and he with Me" –Rev 3:20

"Ask, and it will be given to you; seek, and you will find; knock, and it will be opened to you" –Mt 7:7

"Christ at Hearts Door"
Warner Sallmann

The Door

My father's prayer card given at his wake
showed Jesus knocking at a wooden door
without a handle— because it would take
the soul inside to open it, ask for
the Lord to enter. After my dad died,
I stood against a doorpost, held that card—
and leaned, to gather strength, after I'd cried.
"I am the door. Enter in*." It is hard
to speak through tears, so at those times when all
is dark or pain— just lean on Him. And heed
his knock, then use your knuckles on the wall
to answer when your voice is cracked with need.
You're wordless. Let your body be the prayer.
Your hands are all you need to find Him there.

* *"I am the door. If anyone enters by Me, he will be saved..."* –
Jn 10:9

The day after my father's funeral, my dad's father knew how quiet it would be for my mother and I. My paternal grandfather, who I called Poppy, said it was always hardest after the busy-ness had passed, after the way we labored to help make my father's wake and funeral meaningful, after we were nourished by the Sacraments, and had been given comfort by all who loved us... well, the next day would be painfully quiet. He wasn't wrong. We woke up the day after the burial, in the House of the Sacred Heart and almost didn't know what to do with ourselves with no mourners to greet, or errands to run. Before I could summon the resolve to appear at the breakfast table, I was overtaken by a silent flood of tears and leaned against the heavy, wooden door of the guest bedroom to gather my strength. We are asked to carry some heavy crosses in this world. *"Take up your cross and follow me,"* Jesus instructs us in Matthew 16:24. But we see in Scripture that when Simon carries the heavy cross, it had already been carried by Jesus. I believe it was the Precious Blood of Our Lord, already upon the wood, which gave Simon the strength to walk. When we carry our own cross, let us remember it has already been carried by Christ. Like Simon, we may help move the salvific work of Our Lord forward even if only a few steps by aligning our suffering to His. May we remember that the Most Precious Blood of Our Lord is already on the heavy cross we must carry, and it is that which gives us the strength to forge ahead.

As I leaned in the lintel of the bedroom door and tears overtook me, I recall holding in my hand the prayer card given out at my father's wake. My mother had chosen it: the cover was an image of Jesus knocking at a door, his head gently tilted ever so slightly as though listening for a response on the other side. *"Knock and the door shall be opened,"* we are taught in Matthew 7:7. But of course, it is always God who knocks first, always waiting for our knock to resound, like an echo of his, returning His love. I held that prayer card in my anxious hand.

The Door

I was holding it still when my paternal grandparents arrived at the Red House, along with my grandfather's sister, Sr. A. My grandfather announced he would take my mom and me, along with Nanabelle, out for a nice lunch to break up our somber day and give us the chance to spend time with Sr. A. while she was still in town.

Sr. A. was a living legend: a tenacious Josephite nun, from Brooklyn, New York, who had founded and directed a school in Puerto Rico, in a poor barrio atop a mountain, inaccessible from the main road. The locals called her "the Mother Teresa of Puerto Rico." She was born just two weeks after the miracle at Fatima, and family legend held she was meant to be called Mary de Lourdes, but the pastor instead baptized her Anita de Lourdes, insisting with a biblical cadence that was the child's true name. The beautiful Puerto Rican name she bore inspired her to make a difference there. And so, when she arrived in Ponce as a nun and witnessed the despondency of the poorest of the poor who lived on the mountain, she decided to found a school there. And just as Scripture tells of great transfigurations occurring on mountain tops, her school became a place of deep and abiding change. High on a mountain, this Catholic mission school gave the children who entered it a free Catholic education and a chance for a future.

Known by locals as "the Mayor of the Mountain," Sr. A. would teach by day at the school, and at night hail the locals from her balcony, checking on everyone's well-being. Leaning on her cane, she trekked through the steep slums, visiting and caring for the sick. Beyond ensuring that each of her students would have a solid meal each day and a clean uniform to wear, Sr. A. even helped their parents to find employment.

I was blessed to know Sr. A. as my warm-hearted aunt, and loved her sparkling eyes and resonant laugh. I took her name for Confirmation and won a children's essay contest writing of her courage. One year, as she entered a polling place to vote, a group of thugs approached her with raised fists and tried to block her way. The indomitable nun stood tall and clenched her cane with a steady hand. In a strong, unwavering voice, she said, "I am an American woman. I am here to vote. Let me pass." She spoke with the authority of one of God's faithful soldiers. They got out of her way.

When my great-aunt, Sr. A., entered the Red House, dressed in her bright white habit, her very presence was a comfort. Her skin, tanned golden-brown from her daily walks up and down the mountain, seemed to radiate the sun. Her tall frame was sturdy and strong, despite the ever-present silver cane she leaned on. Her blue eyes still sparkled joyfully even as they welled with sorrow for us, as she leaned against the doorway of the guest bedroom where we were folding laundry. "I'm praying for you all," she said. With those words and the action of blessing she promised, she lifted the cross off my shoulders for a bit. My aunt didn't know that earlier that day I had leaned against the lintel of that same door and cried for my father. But what I didn't know was that in Puerto Rico where Sr. A. prayed nightly for the poor she tended each day; she had a very special door; you might even say, a door to God.

Whenever the school needed repairs or funds, or when someone she loved was in crisis, Sr. A. would open the door to a little closet that she affectionately called her "chapel," and close it behind her. She'd tug the pull-chain that turned on the overhead lightbulb, then would face the simple crucifix and kneel down on a rickety old kneeler, praying for help. Her sister nuns and the lay missionaries who worked with her recount that in the morning as she made her favorite treat, Puerto Rican coffee with cream, her eyes would sparkle almost mischievously as she'd describe her long and arduous prayers of the night before. "I had such a long talk with Him," she'd say between sips. "I was with Him all night and I told Him all about it. He knows." Miraculously, help always seemed to come from somewhere. I often think that my ability to come through that hard time must have had something to do with her constant prayers.

On the back of my father's wake prayer card it says this:

"Father, we pray that nothing of our life will be lost, but that it will be of benefit to the world; that all that we hold sacred may be respected by those who follow us. We ask You that we may go on living in our family and friends, in their hearts and minds, their courage and their conscience. 'We have loved them dearly during life, let us not abandon them until we have conducted them by our prayers into the house of the Lord.' -St. Ambrose"

I feel my aunt was a vigilant prayer champion. And thinking of how she looked at me, with those steel blue eyes, surrounded by laugh lines, yet resolute; I am sure she opened that door to her prayer cell many a night with my family's healing in her heart.

These days, my favorite nightly prayer is the Efficacious Novena to the Sacred Heart of Jesus. It was given to me by a priest who knew Padre Pio. It was St. Pio's favorite nightly prayer, and praying it is a way to remain connected to Padre Pio. The prayer includes these words, "O my Jesus, you have said: 'Truly I say to you, ask and you will receive, seek and you will find, knock and it will be opened to you.' Behold I knock, I seek and ask..." It was amazing to realize the beloved Sacred Heart prayer of one of my favorite saints is so closely connected with my father's prayer card.

May we, like Sr. A. of Ponce, Puerto Rico, open the doors to both our prayer cells and our hearts with frequency and urgency. May we, like her, become exhilarated with the trust that comes from the exertion of tenacious prayer to the Sacred Heart of Jesus, the abyss of all virtues. May we ask, may we seek, may we knock!

Ponder and Pray

- Where do you go to pray alone?

- What is a running theme in your conversations with the Lord?

- What is a "doorway" to prayer for you? For example: a prayer upon waking; grace before meals; the Angelus at noon; 3:00 Divine Mercy prayer; at Mass; or a prayer right before bedtime?

Let us pray the Efficacious / Unfailing Novena Prayer to the Sacred Heart

O Jesus, You said, "In truth I tell you, ask and you shall receive, seek and you shall find, knock and it will open!" I am knocking, seeking and asking for the grace... and I will know You always more intimately.

Sacred Heart of Jesus, I trust in You!

O Jesus, You said, "In truth I tell you, whatever you ask from My Father in My Name, He will grant you!" I ask this grace ... from Your Father and in Your Name and that I may love You and make You loved always more ardently.

Sacred Heart of Jesus, I trust in You!

O Jesus, You said, "In truth I tell you, the heavens and earth will pass away, but My words never!" Counting on the infallibility of Your holy words, I ask for the grace ... and to imitate and serve You always more faithfully.

Sacred Heart of Jesus, I trust in You!

O Jesus, for whom nothing is impossible except not to have compassion for the unhappy, have mercy on us poor sinners, and grant us the grace we ask, through the intercession of the Immaculate Heart of Mary, Your and our tender Mother. Amen.

Heart of Jesus, King and Center of all hearts, have mercy on us.

"David the Shepherd"
Elizabeth Jane Gardner

The Lesson of
The Psalmist

A Despairing Lament: "Lord, the God of my salvation, I call out by day; at night I cry aloud in your presence. Let my prayer come before you; incline your ear to my cry." –Psalm 88:2-3

"King David Playing the Harp"
Gerard van Honthorst

When The Light Went Out: A Psalm

O Lord, my grief was folded like a fleece
across my bed at night, delaying rest.
Afraid of nightmares, restless, wanting peace,
I'd tug the blankets, waiting for the blessed
saltwater stain of sleep upon my lips.
And hours would pass before sleep came. That's how
I tucked myself in every night. The ships
I dreamed of were my father. Every prow
his neck, O Lord. Each sail, his hair. Enough,
to be rocked by him. Yet he stood on deck
beside me, made of warm, still-solid stuff.
Awakening, there was only the wreck.
Sweet memories of him were like a ghost—
the fleece I wore by day, skimming the coast.

The fleece of grief I wore, skimming the coast,
you know, Heavenly Father. How adrift
my heart felt: wrecked, unmoored. The Holy Ghost
pursued me as I drifted, gave the gift
of fortitude: a dwelling place of strength
that came through authenticity in prayer.
I cannot keep you, O Lord, at arm's length,
Your Heart burns through my darkness like a flare
of rescue. On my knees before you, pain
and anger melt before your fiery love.
Rescue me, O lord; Lift me up, sustain
me with the Bread of Life. Send me the dove
that holds the olive branch to bring me calm.
I want for all my life to be your psalm.

Faithful Fortitude is a phrase I use to describe Nanabelle. Faithful fortitude is the only thing that makes authentic joy possible. Fortitude is mental and emotional strength in facing difficulty; it's one of the seven gifts of the Holy Spirit, and it has the added bonus of containing the word "fort" within. Our matriarch was a true fort, a home I could go to, a person who gave without hesitating in my times of need. And how often did she herself face a difficulty, and always with mental and emotional strength?

But what gives this quality of fortitude its light and grace is the faith that makes it possible. For Nanabelle was not strong because she was invulnerable. She was strong because her faith ran deep, so deep that she passed it down to all her children, no easy task in a secular world. In the wake of my painful childhood loss, she was a fort of fortitude for me, deepening my faith even when it was tested.

The Sunday after my father's funeral, Nanabelle set about getting ready for Mass. My mother had gone to an earlier Mass so she could attend to some necessary tasks. My grandmother was ready to drive us to church and I still hadn't come down the stairs. She called out, "I'll be waiting for you in the car. Lock the door behind you when you leave."

I was dressed in my Sunday best as was my family's custom, but I still didn't feel ready. I had not slept much the night before, or really any night since my father's funeral. I'd watch the painful hours pass on the digital clock in the guest bedroom of my grandmother's house, where I slept in the white wrought-iron bed beneath a framed pencil drawing of Jesus holding a lost sheep; the Savior's hand wound prominent as he held the lamb close to His heart. My dreams were sorrowful and on the worst nights, I wept in my sleep, as though my very soul was trying to call for my father. Upon opening my eyes, feeling unrested and groggy, I was

146

immediately assaulted by memories and the ache of grief would return. So when I met my grandmother in the car, I said not a word as I shut the heavy car door. The noise it made as it closed echoed between us, and then after a pause, she spoke.

"What's wrong? You've been quiet all morning," she said.

"I don't really... want to go," I stammered, "I'm feeling... I don't know...angry, lost, just awful."

She paused a long while. I didn't know what she might say. I was feeling very far from God and the thought of going to church seemed almost foreign. I did not want to stand and kneel and sit. I wanted my father; the earthly one. I did not know what to say or do before the Heavenly King. I longed to find the right words to convey what I was feeling, but I said nothing more. Finally, she spoke.

"Well... I'm mad, too," she said. "Why don't we go to church together and talk to God about it?"

I felt a burden lift from my shoulders. She had really heard me and acknowledged my pain, then given me a solution: to choose honesty before God, sharing my heart with Him, remaining in close relationship with Him rather than hiding away, lost in my own pain.

"Okay. Let's do that," I answered her.

As Nanabelle and I sat together in church and the Psalm for that Sunday was sung, Psalm 147: "Bless the Lord, My Soul, who heals the broken-hearted," I heard the outcry of the psalmist, boldly telling of a broken heart and calling out to God in prayer, and with every word that was sung, it resonated in me that sharing one's pain honestly could be part of a worthy prayer.

As she and I knelt together in prayer, side by side, and I silently gave voice in prayer to my lamentation, as I started to tell God of my anger, any walls I had started to build around my heart fell down. The anger dissolved to love. As Mother Teresa says, "I have found the paradox that if you love until it hurts, then there is no hurt, only more love." This lesson from my grandmother solidified the authenticity of faith for me, the fact that I never need hide or pretend before God, but in the manner of David the Psalmist, confide anything in prayer.

Ponder and Pray

• Have you ever experienced desolation in prayer? What eventually turned it around?

• What person in your life has embodied fortitude for you?

Let us pray

You invite all who are burdened to come to You.
Allow Your healing hand to heal me.
Touch my soul with Your compassion for others.
Touch my heart with Your courage and infinite love for all.
Touch my mind with Your wisdom, that my mouth may always
proclaim your praise.
Teach me to reach out to You in my need, and help me to lead
others to You by my example.
Most loving Heart of Jesus, bring me health in body and spirit
that I may serve You with all my strength.
Touch gently this life which You have created, now and forever.
Amen.

Heart of Jesus, in Whom are all the treasures of wisdom and knowledge, have mercy on us.

"The Holy Spirit as a dove in the Heavenly Trinity through the
Incarnation of the Son"
Bartolomé Esteban Murillo

The Lesson of The Blue Willow Plates

"And you are witness of these things. And I send the promise of my Father upon you: but stay you in the city till be endued with power from on high." –Lk 24:48-49

Blue Willow Plates

Those childhood nights I ate at your table,where life's
mysteries were broken and shared—I studied the blue willow
plates you set each night.
Even during the worst winter,
my fork swept potatoes, gravy, bits of savory meat
and uncovered a story.
Each night I told myself a different tale, cast in the familiar
pattern—
there were pagodas, fences, shining waterways
and a boat with a figure searching the horizon.
But what kind of wind made the willow fronds splay so far
apart?
Who were the three figures holding lanterns on a bridge?
And why was the pair of birds larger than the strife below?
You fed me from willow-patterned dishes
when I didn't think I could eat—
when my father was dying, and daffodils were frozen under
snow.
But always on your plates
flying above the relentless searching—
two birds, facing each other, wings arched in triumph.

That winter, in blue and white patterns,
the Holy Spirit, in its many-feathered glory
descended on each dish you placed before me.

I n the months after my father's death, my mother and I spent our days and nights with Nanabelle. The three of us together were pushing forward through this new challenge, our attempt to adjust to life without my father. We would plan our dinner menu and remind one another what each night's television menu offered as well. We had our regular and reliable favorites, always with a cup of tea. During the *Lawrence Welk Show* we would choose our favorite singers, dancers, skits and other performances of the evening. As we watched *Murder She Wrote*, we tried to guess the bad guy, looking for the clues, and on a lighter side, commenting on Jessica Fletcher's décor and wardrobe. Lifetime's Movie of the Week offered romantic movies and American Movie Classics gave us our favorites, the black and white films of the thirties and forties. Nanabelle would tell us about the actors and actresses of that time. All the British shows were becoming popular on American television at that time, and we looked forward each week to watching the antics of the comedians on *Fawlty Towers, Mr. Bean*, and *Are You Being Served*.

My grandmother and I took particular delight in the ballroom dancing competitions. The dance partners, their rhythmic moves, facial expressions and costumes were all under our careful inspection and given our seal of approval. Sometimes, by myself, I would enjoy an episode of *All Creatures Great and Small*, or *Little House on the Prairie*, shows I had once watched with my father. I would remember him sitting next to me in our Family Room.

Dinner time brought another kind of healing. You already know the great care with which Nanabelle prepared a meal and set a table— well, I learned from her to do the same when I was asked to "get out the plates." Nanabelle's plates were blue-and-white willow china, evoking the color of Mary's mantle and her purity. They made the most simple meal elegant. One vivid memory I have is of a meal that Nana served me on those plates when I first stayed there on my own, when my father was dying. The scene on my dish drew me into another place. The people on the plate piqued my interest. Perhaps I was encouraged to keep eating, when I really had no appetite, because with each bite the scene on the plate was revealed to me. And so, I set about writing a story of hope from the pictures and actions on the plate as a way to escape the real story I was presently in.

At the top of the scene were two birds in flight, facing each other. Below, there were pagodas, and trees bearing all kinds of fruits and flowers. There were three figures on a bridge carrying lanterns. They were the Father, Son and Holy Spirit, a Trinity of immortal forbearance. There was a lonely traveler on a fishing boat. The three on the bridge with lights were there to aid the traveler.

In the original story, I believe, the three figures on the bridge were meant to signify trouble for the traveler, but I didn't see it that way at all. The soaring birds and the trees swaying in the wind signified the presence of the Holy Spirit surrounding and leading the action. The tree in the foreground reveals its sturdy roots acting as a dome for the three on the bridge.

It was clear by the swaying branches of the trees that there was a storm going on. And yet the birds were larger than the strife below.

Ponder and Pray

- In the house of the Sacred Heart the meals were given out of love and care by Nanabelle and served on blue willow plates. The deeper meaning of the plate was the work of a child's imagination and the Spirit, working with Nanabelle. Did you ever help someone and find that added blessings came from your efforts that were not in your control (you were the catalyst... then the Spirit took over)? Explain.

- What does the kitchen and/or things in the kitchen mean to you in your life?

- How do you explain that the plates gave comfort during this dreadful time?

Let us pray: O Lord Jesus Christ, to Your most Sacred Heart, I confide this intention (state it). Only look upon me, then do what Your love inspires. Let Your Sacred Heart decide... I count on You... I trust in You... I throw myself on Your mercy. Lord, Jesus, You will not fail me.

Sacred Heart of Jesus, I trust in You.

Sacred Heart of Jesus, I believe in Your love for me.

Sacred Heart of Jesus, Your kingdom come.

Sacred Heart of Jesus, I have asked You for many favors, but I earnestly implore this one. Take it, place it in Your open Heart. When the Eternal Father looks upon it, He will see it covered with Your Precious Blood. It will be no longer my prayer, but Yours, Jesus. Sacred Heart of Jesus, I place all my trust in You. Let me not be disappointed.

Amen.

Heart of Jesus, in Whom dwells the fullness of Divinity, have mercy on us.

"The Virgin Mary Receiving the Eucharist from Saint John the Apostle"
John Flemish School

The Lesson of The Kitchen

"They ate together with glad and sincere hearts."
–Acts 2:46

The House of the Sacred Heart

In the house of the Sacred Heart,
from which we're called to never part,
there are mysteries of joy and pain—
where the warmest days bring the hardest rain;
at life's truest moments, it is there we have lain.
There is family in the house of the Sacred Heart
who have taught us the meaning of a blessed day.
Their journeys cross ours — and point the way.
Ancestors, saints, family and friends—
pray for us till this journey ends.

This house is the place we'll always keep
The memories that never sleep—
The poignant love that runs so deep.
Each of us has rested our head
in trust upon our God and Bread.
In the house of the Sacred Heart,
from which we're called to never part,
there are mysteries of joy and pain—
where the warmest days bring the hardest rain;
at life's truest moments, it is there we have lain.

Life without my father and Grandpapa was sorrowful—overwhelmingly so, and not just for me. I understood that it was a dark time for everyone who came and went from the Red House, and never more so than the week after my father's funeral. The kitchen of the Red House became the haven for all as we tried to navigate these unfamiliar, stormy seas. All of us were numb and mourning in our own ways, and yet, all drew strength from each other, from our rich faith and from the mysteries of healing that came from our shared home... the Red House.

That Red House was founded on the rock, the rock of St. Peter: our Catholic faith. That is the only rock that keeps a person safe in all the storms of life, even when the church itself is enduring an age of challenges, the gates of hell will never prevail against it (that doesn't mean it won't rough it up a bit first). And so, during our formative experience of suffering, the gates of hell did not prevail.

A few days after my father's funeral, my aunts and uncles gathered at the Red House for a family meeting, to see how my mom and I were faring and to strengthen each other. Hugs and kisses were exchanged and coats were hung as all settled into their usual places in the kitchen while my grandmother served the cold cuts, potato salad, and crumb cake. As they poured their tea they exchanged stories of the wake, funeral and the gathering afterward that had been hosted at the Red House.

Each one of them had a teacup before them, steam of the hot brew rising up, like incense before prayer. Teacups in my family came to represent for me the means to working out almost any problem. The kitchen we gathered in to break bread and open our hearts was our very own Cenacle, our own "Upper Room," returning to a place that gave all of us sustenance when we knew not what else to do. As I sat in the kitchen with all of them, I saw each one's personality symbolized in the objects they sat near.

My Aunt G spoke first, interrupting the din of chatter and starting our meeting. She was sitting underneath a line drawing of a pitcher with the words "On the Strength of the Word of the Woman" quoting the scriptural account of the Woman at the Well. As she spoke, it was as though she was drawing from the well of our Lord's mercy. "Annabelle, I'd like you and your mom to come up soon to our home for an overnight trip. We'll take you to the zoo, shop and go to lunch. We're here for you. Whatever you two need, you can always call us. But let's make sure we make these plans official as something for you to look forward to."

On the Strength of the Word of the Woman

To GBS

> "You shall draw waters with joy out of the Saviour's fountains" Is 12:3

In the kitchen of my grandmother's house,
when sorrow came, so did the women—
ready to heal, but first, to talk.
In a circle, around the table,
a ring of conversation, consolation.
To the child I was, in the midst of the winter of loss—
we were entertaining angels.

Their words were filigreed with steam
from the cups of tea before them.
I listened and sometimes joined in—
strengthened by their voices, and the teapot's reverent bow
over the prayers between our words — *Dear God, what can we do?*
Help us. Show us how to be of use.

The women's voices and stories, tears and laughter
offset the pain. There were light-catchers hanging
on the bay window of the kitchen—
and they might as well have been the stained glass
of an ornate church. Our words bounced off their brightness
and the spectrum of colors tinged the tablecloth.

My aunt, my grandmother's first child
sat in the chair beneath a framed print—
Line drawing of a pitcher,
its mouth ready to draw water,
its one arched handle like a listening ear.
Atop the pitcher were these words:
On the strength of the word of the woman.

On the pitcher, in calligraphy, attributes of a good woman:
courage, faithfulness, love—
My grandmother's reminder to all the girls who followed
of what we were called to be: women strong in the Word
drawing living water from His Heart.

My aunt who sat beneath the pitcher
was always ready to pour herself out like a libation—
Though she lived the farthest away,
she would journey whenever needed—
to fill what was empty,
wash what was sore,

complete our circle around that table,
and anoint, with her presence—
the strength of the words of the women.

"Jesus and the Samaritan Woman"
Veronese

When Uncle B. heard Aunt G's offer to take my mother and I to the zoo, he chimed in, "Can I come?" And we all laughed. He offered, without missing a beat, "I want to take you two up to the ski resort and get you on the slopes. And by the way, Annabelle, I'll be driving you to school from now on." He was sitting in the rocker beneath the antique clock and as the pendulum ticked and the rocker swayed, I could feel him balancing my life into a hope for normalcy, a return to the regular rhythm of things.

The Regulator

for BTB

> "A time to weep and a time to laugh; a time to
> mourn and a time to dance" Eccl 3:4

The Regulator was the antique clock
my grandmother had on her kitchen wall.
Its golden pendulum with every tock
was like her house's pulse, a constant call
to life. Always in motion, steady, strong—
my uncle would stop by many a night
to join us for a meal. A joke or song
was ever on his lips. He was the light—
a constancy of goodness I could trust
when grief had left us numb, and time was locked.
His presence, like a gear shifting the dust—
marking delight the moment that he knocked.
Despite the painful hours he would face,
Our Regulator balanced all with grace.

Uncle E. was sitting on the antique milk can beneath the country wall calendar to the right of the dishwasher. After Uncle B. described his willingness to drive me to school each day, as a steady companion along the journey, everyone started talking excitedly and the many voices melding together grew louder and more animated. Then, in a calm, low voice, Uncle E. brought a peaceful tone as he revealed his plan to us. He said, "You're invited to join our summer vacation by the seaside this July for some much-needed rest and sunshine." He was silent for a while and then added, "I think we need a new tradition. Consider yourself invited to the summer place every year. We'll be there a whole month. You can stay as much of that time as you'd like. There's nothing like being by the sea." At that, Uncle G. started snapping his fingers and the uncles launched into a spontaneous rendition of Bobby Darin's "Beyond the Sea." Singing at any opportunity was a trademark of my uncles.

The Harmonizer

for EFB

"Sing to the Lord with Thanksgiving; with the lyre make music to our God." Psalm 147:7

In my grandmother's crowded kitchen,
as family gathered, even in hard times—
the uncles would break into song.
I would listen to my middle uncle's harmony.
His resonant tone was enough to bring peace—
and an agelessness transcending cares.

He, the philosopher, would sit on the antique milk can,
one arm leaning on the butcher block counter—
the country calendar hanging above him.
The songs and the years would collide.
I'd almost hear the ghost chords of his childhood guitar
echoing from the second floor.
As he sang, we were brought to one accord.
A chant of hymns resounding in his veins,
he'd sing the *mysterium tremendum*
of God and creation. His place in things:
the tenor in a choir of praise.

"Angel Playing the Lute"
Rosso Firentino

As my uncles' song subsided, my mother and I were laughing. We would not have thought laughter possible in such somber days, but there we were, our sides hurting from such unexpected levity. It was my mother who spoke next. "You're giving us both so much hope," she said, "We love you all and we will always be there to help each of you as well."

The Gift of Hope

for AMR

> "Hope is the thing with feathers that perches in the soul and sings the tune without the words and never stops at all." -Emily Dickinson

Grandmother's shelf that held Depression glass,
and porcelain cups (a contrast side-by-side,
of times to savor; times you wish would pass)
had a hand-painted plaque hanging beside
and it was crafted by my mother's hand,
a gift she gave for Father's Day one year
to try to help her father understand
the way he'd taught his family to revere,
and hope in God. She'd painted him a dove
flying on top, the Holy Spirit, lines
by Dickinson about the tune of love
God sings unceasingly. She painted signs
like this for each loved one's home, handmade gift
for all who seeing it, felt their hope lift.

For all who seeing it, felt their hope lift—
and this was what my mother always gave:
the gift of beauty. Beauty was the gift.
She'd scrub and clean, know what to toss and save,
hang pictures, and paint murals on the wall,
polish and sort, then decorate and shine.
She'd bring order and then arrange a sprawl
of roses. To her, home was like a shrine,
a church. Her efforts made you want to stay.
She knew the Sacred Heart dwelled in her home
and that is why she served others that way.
She'd turn a domicile into a dome
of hope. And like her Father, gone before,
she knew labor was beauty, not a chore.

"Tea"
Mary Cassat

The Kitchen

Uncle G. who had been awaiting the best moment for his turn to speak, was standing in the kitchen doorway, under the wooden beam that ran the length of the kitchen, and leaning against the wall. He reached into his jacket and pulled out a card, handing it to my mother. "There's some cash in there for you," he told her. "It's to buy Annabelle some new rollerblades. You know, she doesn't have a dad to keep her active and having fun so I want to help out. Rollerblades are the new thing all the kids are doing and she'll love it. Take her to the sporting good store and buy her a pair of skates on me. And I'll be checking in now and then to see her progress."

Nanabelle laughed from her seat at the table. "What'll they think of next? In my day it was roller skates and I loved it. This will be fun."

I embraced Uncle G, delighted by his gift, and while I was up from my seat gave hugs all around.

The Beam

for GB

"The Lord supports all who are falling and raises up
all who are bowed down." Ps 145:14

In my grandmother's house, running across
the kitchen ceiling was a wooden beam.
As though from Joseph's workshop, or the cross
the Savior carried uphill to redeem
the world, it was an emblem of support.
My uncle often stood beneath its span
and leaned against the wall. He was a fort
of tenderness and strength. He'd have a plan
to fix things; to repair the antique home;
rescue the shattered scheme; bolster the weight
of pain with words of praise. He was the dome
who'd hold you up, but also renovate.
Although he labored to repair and mend,
this beam held firm each person he would tend.

"Christ Carrying the Cross"
Circle of Giovanni Bellini

Lastly, Aunt B. spoke saying, "Hold on, I have something to say, too. I just want you both to know you won't be alone. If you ever want company, I'll be around... you won't be able to get rid of me! We can go to movies, have dinner, just get together for a cup of tea, and talk. Whatever you want to do, I'm here for you." These words were a consolation, as though she had shone light into our darkness. She was always helping family members, and true to her word that she would not leave someone she loved alone, years later it would be she who gave Nanabelle a home when my grandmother was too old to live alone any longer.

The Light Catcher

for BBK

> "You are the light of the world. A city set on a
> mountain can not be hidden. Nor do they light a
> lamp and then put it under a bushel basket; it is set
> on a lampstand, where it gives light to all in the
> house." Mt 5:14-15

The rain had ended, and all at once,
sunlight streamed through the stained glass light-catcher
which graced the kitchen window.
It bore your family name and the Claddagh:
the hands and crowned heart,

The Kitchen

their green and gold tones
coloring the tablecloth
with reminders of friendship, loyalty and love.

You sat beside at the table,
steeping the tea in the blue and white pot—
and knowing the time had come.

"You won't be alone," you said.
There were daisies in a green vase
at the table's center, where you sat—
and that sudden burst of light, bright as prayer.

But there was no winged apparition before your assent.
One day, my aunt, you were hailed with understanding—
the aging woman who'd birthed and sheltered you
could no longer live alone— so you said yes.
You poured a cup, and gave it to your mother.

There was no way to know
of her coming fall,
the surgery, new pins in the hip—
her learning to walk anew the way she once taught you—
the *Anima Christi* she would say boldly
in the face of darkness.

Your nod said *let it be done unto me—*
yes to the tide of fear and hope
that would make your home into a small boat
riding a strange ocean, unable to see
a hand before you in the night.

You and she would take turns getting out of the boat—
stepping on foam-capped breakers,
reaching for the One who walks the waves
even when you feared the sea would swallow you up.

The yes you said rimmed the bow and stern,
the mast and sail in stars—
the yes you said became a constellation.

The yes you said became a constellation
to give your family light—
The Light-Catcher, you.
And the light you caught was your mother,
the Centenary Saint who prayed: *Soul of Christ, be my
sanctification*—
gave the younger ones an example to witness, to follow—
that life is dignity at every stage,
that caring for ancestors is as fierce a privilege as caring for
descendants.

You won't be alone, you said.

The yes you said is your Annunciation—
and the soul of Christ is in your star-rimmed home.

"The Annunciation"
Henry Ossawa Tanner

Ponder and Pray

- What family members were key players in your formative years or are in your life now? Can you think of an object that might symbolize them?

- What object in your kitchen best describes you and the contributions you made to your loved ones?

Let us pray Prayer to the Sacred Heart of Jesus

Most Sacred Heart of Jesus, pour down Your blessings abundantly on Your holy Church, on the Supreme Pontiff, and on all the clergy. Grant perseverance to the just, convert sinners, enlighten infidels, bless our parents, friends, and benefactors, assist the dying, free the souls in purgatory, and extend over all hearts the sweet empire of Your love.

- Indulgence of 300 days, once a day - Pope Pius X, 16 June 1906

Heart of Jesus, in Whom the Father was well pleased, have mercy on us.

"Christ at the home of Martha and Mary"
Henryk Siemiradzki

The Lesson of The Bethany Cook

"Now as they went on their way, he entered a certain village, where a woman named Martha welcomed him into her home. She had a sister named Mary, who sat at the Lord's feet and listened to what he was saying." –Lk 10:38-39

"Christ in the House of Martha and Mary"
Johannes Vermeer

Martha

Since Christ Himself was visiting my house,
I wanted to prepare my greatest dish.
I labored at the stove and meant to douse
the lamb with wine; instead, I drowned the fish.
"He might have let me know when he'd drop by,"
I whispered as I swept the kitchen clean,
and I let out a pitiable sigh.
Where was my sister Mary in this scene?
I searched, and found her sitting at Christ's feet,
delighted by each story that he'd start.
I asked if she would help me serve the meat,
but Jesus said she'd picked the better part.
And so I joined my sister at his side—
and Jesus took the burned meal quite in stride.

For the years without Grandpapa, Nanabelle found new traditions. One was that on Christmas Eve, whoever was alone for the holiday was invited to her house for dinner. It was always fried shrimp and spaghetti. Sometimes, a family member would bring along another pilgrim who they thought could use some "food for the journey." It was always a cheerful evening, full of joy in the brightly decorated rooms. Needless to say, my mom and I were present at many of these dinners and often helped Nanabelle to prepare for them. But honestly, there were many she prepared all by herself. Her touches were evident everywhere, right down to the blue willow plates and red glassware. Prayer was always part of the evening in the beautiful and personal grace before meals and a welcome to everyone present.

I always marveled that despite how hard she worked on these special dinners, from the savory food to the elegant table settings, Nanabelle also managed to be fully present to her guests. She'd laugh and chatter away, but was as good a listener as she was a talker, and friends often remarked how she made them feel heard. She was very present to each person with whom she spoke. She often tucked her chin on her hand as she nodded.

What I have come to realize is that my grandmother had mastered the art of balancing serving and socializing, of both laboring for and listening to her guests. In so doing, she made each person feel important and taken care of. She was the best blend of Martha and Mary, the two sisters in Scripture who entertain Jesus at their home in Bethany which was such a valued haven for him. Scripture teaches that Jesus felt at home with them in Bethany. One can imagine that after his gentle lesson that Mary "had chosen the better part," Martha would have learned to better manage to balance the full plate of cooking and keeping conversation. And so, my grandmother was a Bethany Cook, a phrase I coined to explain the beautiful blend of host and partaker that we are all called to master; and she was able to personify.

Hanging in her kitchen was the poem I had written about Martha. She laughed to read that Martha burned her meal while trying to be more present to Jesus. My grandmother always had a great sense of humor, and perhaps it was this that helped her balance both roles with such grace and humility. She ended every day asking, in her own words, "How did I goof today, Lord? What do you need me to do better tomorrow?"

What was it about that house in Bethany that made Jesus feel so at home? I can only imagine that the siblings who lived there had a blend of good humor, good food, and good conversation, and made their home a house for... and of, the Sacred Heart.

Ponder and Pray

- Recall some of the most memorable meals shared with friends and loved ones.

- Can you remember some of the most nourishing conversations you've taken part in? What comes to mind? Who are the people you can rely on for such a dining experience?

- What is the difference in the experiences between a meal eaten without prayer versus one with a meaningful grace

- Can you think of a time when you showed hospitality and you know it made a difference?

Let us pray: Eternal Father, I offer the Sacred Heart of Jesus with all its love, all its sufferings of and all its merits:

First - To expiate all the sins I have committed this day and during all my life. (Glory Be)

Second - To purify the good I have done badly this day and during all my life. (Glory Be.)

Third - To supply for the good I ought to have done and I have neglected this day and during all my life. (Glory Be.)

Heart of Jesus, of Whose fullness we have all received, have mercy on us.

"Christ with Mary and Martha"
Jacopo Tintoretto

"Trees and Undergrowth"
Vincent van Gogh

The Lesson of
The Birchbark

"The dead man came out, tied hand and foot with burial bands, and his face was wrapped in a cloth. So Jesus said to them, 'Untie him and let him go.'" –Jn 11:44

Birch Bark

My uncle brought me the skin of trees
as an empty manuscript—
(shed, husked scales
gathered from woods,
fallen footnotes of birch bark)
with dark grace notes
like type on white paper.
He placed them in a canvas bag,
gave them to the child I was, said,
Write your poems on these.
Tonight, in this dusk-spilled forest
all is green—
dusty ground, foal-warm—
air, pond-cool.
I remember first poems.
They, like scrawled henna on wrists of wood—
silent pulse waiting beneath,
pictographs of what I hoped to reveal.

I still seek to translate
the grains of wood he gathered,
find the language—
splintered hieroglyphs he left—
meaning encoded there.
Each word he never spoke
was laid to rest with him
and if even one of them
falls from my fingers
as night inks the woods
in stillness—
one tree-ring is added to this book.

My mother's uncle T., a priest, was a beloved member of the House of the Sacred Heart. He was Nanabelle's oldest brother. They were the first son and daughter of ten children and were very close. Both were smart and shared similar temperaments. His visits were a great healing during the years that followed the loss of my father and grandfather. Nanabelle and Uncle T. had great talks over coffee and crumb buns, and he loved to stay for dinner because Nanabelle cooked like their mother. Sometimes, he'd stay for several days, even at times up to two weeks. He did much to nourish her soul during these visits, talking about faith and family. And I might add, Nanabelle did much to recharge her brother's spirits. They would laugh a lot and reminisce. The House of the Sacred Heart was reinvigorated during these visits and Nanabelle was well-aware of her importance in her brother's life.

My uncle lived at the Shrine of the Martyrs at Auriesville, upstate New York. Along with being a retreat leader and spiritual advisor there, he humbly cut the lawn and gardened the cemetery of the priests. He used to say with a smile, that he was tending his final resting place. My uncle was a saintly man; he had been imprisoned for his faith as a young missionary in the Philippines during World War II.

He had been there to teach the faith to Filipino children. A few months before he was scheduled to return home to the United States, the Japanese invaded the island. He was captured and imprisoned in a war camp. While there, he noticed that when the food was given, hungry adult prisoners ate the children's food. He heroically gave his meager bowl of rice to the children, but he only had one bowl to share. So, entertaining his captors by playing his violin, he negotiated with them to be allowed to be the prisoners' cook, and that way, he was able to portion out the food, ensuring the children had enough to eat. When he was finally freed at war's end, he suffered from malaria, had missing teeth, and had lost much weight. No wonder, then, that my grandmother loved to feed him. Until her dying day she kept as one of her most treasured possessions the letter he sent home to his family the day he was freed from the war camp. Here is the text of that letter:

Dear Family,

It's so great that I marvel that I can get myself together as much as this to write a letter. What I've been awaiting for three long hungry years has taken me by surprise and I can hardly believe it. I can't say much, I just have a lump in my throat. I don't know how to behave. Here I am smoking an American cigarette and in my stomach a pot of pork and beans, the first time I have had enough to eat in this camp. It's like Heaven – freedom – a new world – and very worthwhile fighting for. I have no shoes. One of my two shirts is on me. A pair of shorts complete my outfit. I have neither plate, nor knife nor fork. My eating gear is a rusty spoon and two tin cans, but I'm happy.

The boys are here, their guns are booming away, Manila is blowing up and burning like hell, the enemy's on the run, I'm writing home and today they are listing the names of those who wish to return to the states. I'm happy and I'm sure you'll be glad to know that of all the men here, I have stood it best. I am in better health than any of them. I tip the scales at 155 lbs. No limbs are missing. I am whole save that I lost two teeth that broke off at the root when I struck a stone while eating rice. The dentist said I am so run down that my teeth just cannot stand a little shock like that.

Of course, I have plenty to tell you about but I am going to leave that to following letters. The main thing now is to let you know that I am alive and well. The one package and four or five letters I received from you were addressed to me at Davao. I am under the impression that you think I am still there dead or alive; but no. We were taken out of there on Christmas eve, 1943- I have had no sleep for three nights- must finish this letter for a rush mail tonight and in a few minutes change my quarters.

Oh! I could just ramble on forever but as I said I must get my things together. My love to all of you.

How often I have prayed for you. How often wondered what you will still look like. My captors took away from me, three years ago, what photos I had of you and I found that hard.

I'll see you all soon.

My regards to all my relatives and friends.

Love and oodles of kisses

T

(God bless America land that I love.)

And so, Auriesville, the land where the North American martyrs, Saint Isaac Jogues and his companions, had spread the Gospel and given their lives for God: was a fitting place for my uncle to live. He had a martyr's spirit. When he was just a little boy he told his sister, my grandmother, "I want to be a priest. Think of it; life is short. I'd rather give up my whole life here on earth and dedicate it to God and gain eternity." For three long, hungry years in the Philippines, he was imprisoned for his dedication to God. I still recall the celebration of his 50 year anniversary of priesthood at Auriesville. Our whole family went up and stayed there, overnight, when the foliage was at its peak, in October. Orange, red, and yellow leaves against a bright blue sky, white clouds and evergreen trees were the palette of colors surrounding our prayerful time of celebrating the priesthood of our family's spiritual advisor. He said Mass and gave us a tour of the woods and grounds, emphasizing the great sacrifice of love that had been made there. I was struck by the poetic significance that a man who had been imprisoned for his faith during World War Two, chancing martyrdom, now tended the history and grounds of the site of the North American martyrs, from whose blood the seeds of the American church took root.

On a particular day, about a year after my father's death, Uncle T. visited Nanabelle's Red House and brought gifts for me. First, he gave me Palgrave's Golden Treasury of Poetry. "This is one of my favorite books," he said, "and it's essential for you to have a copy, poet that you are." I inscribed the date on the inside cover of the treasury: April 23, the Feast of St. George, Martyr. Then, he opened a canvas bag that was bursting with a harvest of freshly shed birch bark from the white birches of Auriesville and said, "I take a walk through the forest every day as I say my prayers. White birches shed their bark and it's regenerative, it renews the tree." The way he described it reminded me of Lazarus shedding his burial bands and stepping into his new chance at life. My uncle had painstakingly gathered this shorn skin of trees for me as he walked and prayed. His chin was resolute as he said, in a commanding voice, "Here. Write your poems on these." This was birch bark from the trees of the site of the North American Martyrs in Auriesville, grown on the same ground where the martyrs had shed their blood. What a commission was this. My sage uncle, the good and faithful priest, believed in my work, took it seriously and had given me a deeply poetic gift: something as symbolic to him as it would be to me. With that gift he blessed my vocation to write, and like the birch bark, I felt I was beginning to shed mourning in exchange for mission. After thinking and praying about what to do, I wrote a poem for my father and grandfather upon the birchbark, telling them of my love and how much I missed them. I left the birchbark poem in the woods behind my house, among the leaves, trusting God would relay my message.

Uncle T. used to say he prayed to the Messenger in the Tabernacle to deliver his love to the family he sorely missed during the three years he was a prisoner of war. I now prayed to the Holy Spirit to deliver my love to the family I missed, upon the wind.

Ponder and Pray

- When the birch bark was given, it was a blessing, affirming a call to be a writer. Were you ever given a gift that confirmed for you a particular talent or calling you had, or pointed you to it? What might someone give you to affirm your talent?

- Have you ever given such a gift to someone? What might you give someone you love and admire to affirm their interests or talents?

Let us pray Prayer of Thanksgiving and Praise to the Sacred Heart:

Lord, you deserve all honor and praise, because your love is perfect and your heart sublime.

My heart is filled to overflowing with gratitude for the many blessings and graces you have bestowed upon me and those whom I love.

Forever undeserving, may I always be attentive and never take for granted the gifts of mercy and love that flow so freely and generously from your Sacred Heart.

Heart of Jesus, I adore you.

Heart of Jesus, I praise you.

Heart of Jesus, I thank you.

Heart of Jesus, I love you forever and always.

Amen.

Heart of Jesus, desire of the everlasting hills, have mercy on us.

"The Garden of Gethsemane"
Giorgio Vasari

The Lesson of The Arched Window

"Then Jesus came with them to a place called Gethsemane, and he said to his disciples, 'Sit here while I go over there and pray.' He took along Peter and the two sons of Zebedee, and began to feel sorrow and distress." –Mt 26:36-39

"Christ in Gethsemane"
Heinrich Hoffman

The Agony in the Garden

Within a garden like this we were lost.
Eden was rooted to Gethsemane—
We slept while you kept watch and mourned the cost—
gazing at moonlight through the olive trees.
Your red drops fell, consoling Abel's blood
which once cried out from deep within the earth.
Your tears and sweat baptized and blessed the mud.
Sacrificed slumber would have had great worth.
You'd barred us from nightmares: forbidden fruit
we tasted in our dreams. You gave true bread.
We could have nourished you, provided shoots
of strength for branch-deep weariness. Instead,
we closed our eyes, with everything at stake.
All we'd been asked to do was stay awake.

I am always soul-struck by how the Sorrowful Mysteries of the Rosary begin, within the garden of Gethsemane, where Jesus' agony takes place in a garden reminiscent of Eden, where we lost our way. He knows he will be the one to save us, he feels how painful it will be, he is weighed down by the enormity of all our sins for which he will give his life, and... he is alone. His friends fall asleep.

After my father's death, my mother and I lived for several months with my grandmother, and her house was always pulsing with conversation, visitors, and things to do. When we returned home, it was good for my mother and me to get back, to sort out our life's direction and make the place cozy and lived-in once more. We were a very close duo. But since it was just the two of us alone in the house, at night the sorrow sometimes seemed to engulf the rooms. My greatest worry was for my mother. I was very aware of her painful loss, and how hard she was working as a single parent. As each day folded into dusk, and we prepared for nighttime, my worries for her well-being overtook me. I was, simply put, afraid my mother would die, just as my father had. I could not sleep unless I knew she, first, was asleep; that she wasn't awake crying or up working late.

My favorite nights were when the two of us, like friends at a sleepover, would sit in her bed and talk over the day, laughing. Sometimes while we talked, I'd pat my tired mother's head, and when she would fall asleep, I'd stay in the darkness, gazing out the arched window above her bed. Even widowhood did not stop her from being for me the greatest witness of faith I've ever known. And so, I kept watch, and prayed. I watched the stars and moon as I listened to the sound of my mother's breathing. As I watched the expanse of sky, the vast firmament through the large, arched window: I studied the mist moving over the face of the moon, the motion of the stars as the hours pressed on, the evergreens trembling in the wind. My thoughts would turn to the Garden of Gethsemane. Jesus had been left alone in his sorrow. I could never get over that. I felt a strong sense of connection to Jesus there, lonely and afraid, and the only one awake. "I wouldn't fall asleep, Jesus. I'd stay awake, I'd comfort you," I'd pray, and hope my prayers would keep him company there, brought through time and space by those same stars to embrace him.

And the truth is, that as I'd keep that quiet vigil, it was Jesus of Gethsemane who stayed awake with me.

Ponder and Pray

- Can you think of a moment in your life in which your suffering and loneliness made you feel closer to Christ, either at the time or upon reflection?

- Is there a place in your home where you feel connected to the heavens... perhaps a spot where you can look out at the stars and moon?

- Think of those for whom you've stayed awake: the child you've watched over through the night; the aged parent you've cared for till dawn; the friend you've worried for and could not sleep... The next time that happens to us, let us offer that sleeplessness to Jesus in the Garden of Gethsemane. Let none of us sleep when Jesus wishes us to stay awake.

Let us pray: Prayer to Jesus in Gethsemane (by Annabelle Moseley)

O Lord, make a vigil of my life, burning brightly as a torch of love, one that might give warmth in the darkness of Mount Olivet, beyond time and space, in the midst of Your agony. Dearest and Most Adorable Heart of Jesus, may I approach You there in that drear garden, fall to my knees and prostrate myself before You, ever-watchful and ever-prayerful. O, sweet joy, to draw near to You in Your agony!

Merciful Savior, let my love for You be wide-awake all the days of my life. May You make of my heart a humble and adoring companion for Your agony. I seek to approach You among the olive trees, offering love and reparation to You in the Garden of Gethsemane as pious Veronica did on the *Via Dolorosa*. I kiss each drop of blood that falls from You to the ground. I listen to Your words. I sit as near as You want me. I cannot sleep. What might I give You to ease Your pain, O Lord? Under moonlight, under stars, in the company of angels, I give You my will, my heart, and my open eyes, open to Your agony and beauty.

With You and to You I pray, Your Will be done. Lord, on those nights when I cannot sleep, may I not waste my wakefulness. May I unite my wakefulness to the Mount of Olives. For all the days of my life, may I stay awake with You in Gethsemane. May I watch and pray. O Lord, make a vigil of my life.

Heart of Jesus, patient and most merciful, have mercy on us.

"The Agony in the Garden"
Gustave Doré

"The Resurrection of Lazarus"
Leon Bonnat

The Lesson of The Cemetery

"He will wipe every tear from their eyes, and there shall be no more death or mourning, wailing or pain." –Rev 21:4

"The Day of the Dead"
William-Adolphe Bouguereau

Planting at Your Grave

It is warm for November
And the earth is dry and brittle,
Starved for flowers.
I have to claw at the grass, pull it back by the hair,
Trek back and forth to the water hose,
Muddy the soil like a child about to make pies.
Your child for only ten years,
I am playing again;
I am sitting on your sun-drenched lap.

I bury my hands in the womb of the dirt,
Picking through the weeds,
Letting myself take root,
And all the time I feel like scratching my way down to you,
But that thought passes
As I step back and see what I've planted—
Purple mums and Gerber daisies.

Still, I want your voice, your hand, your guidance
I want visitation rights
But I'll come when I'm called, Daddy.
Only then.
You should be loving this—
You had to force me to do yardwork,
And here I am with rake and shovel
Tending what I can for you.
Look at these purple mums and Gerber daisies
And see your daughter planted on your grave.

I am not rooted here;
Watch me walk into the world and live.
I am not dead.
Not most of me.

Cemeteries are not everyone's favorite places. Yet my mother and I would make an outing of our visits there. We'd bring gardening tools and gloves, flowers for planting, snacks and a blanket for a picnic. The cemetery where my father and grandfather are buried is particularly beautiful, a pastoral setting with dogwood, oak, and cypress trees, gently rolling hills, and elaborate statues.

My father and grandfather were resting in peace in the same section of the cemetery, their headstones facing each other, so we could beautify both headstones at the same time. My mother had designed both of the headstones. My father's bore a Celtic cross. The epitaph included this verse: "*Those who have taught many to do what is right will shine like the stars forever*" (Dan 12:3) My grandfather's had palms etched in, with the words, "Born to Eternal Life." I recall the walk I would always take from the headstones to the spigot to fill my watering can with water. I would pass so many etched names, and would think of the lives they had lived, and the people they had left behind. I knew some of those family names from my church and neighborhood; I'd been to some of their funerals. There are so many stories intersecting there among the rows: stories of saintly people who lived challenging but noble lives.

It was a Catholic cemetery, and I was comforted by the many statues and etchings of the Sacred Heart of Jesus in particular. There was also a huge statue of Jesus kneeling in Gethsemane, and another section for deceased infants with a large guardian angel. In some ways, a visit to the cemetery almost felt like a visit to a church. A cemetery is an opportunity: a field filled with names to wander through and pray for, a field of reminders to take up our own life to the fullest while we have it.

One day, while we were at the cemetery, my grandmother was with us. She was tending the graves, and as she passed there she heard someone weeping. Nanabelle, being Nanabelle, wandered over to see the woman. The woman was elderly, but sat on the ground in front of a grave, head bowed down, shoulders heaving. Nanabelle had seen her there before, always in tears. My grandmother asked her, "Why are you crying so?" The woman replied, "I miss my husband so much." Nanabelle replied, "Well, do you want to be with him now?" There was no answer. Nanabelle continued, "Well, don't worry. I'm sure you'll be with him soon." The woman stopped crying at once. "I will *not* be with him soon!" she said, and stood, angrily walking away.

Nanabelle always enjoyed telling this story. She knew the advice might have seemed harsh, but was a kindness; for she said that woman wiped her tears and stood with a look of purpose and determination. Nanabelle knew well how one can get lost in sorrow and it can be difficult to find your way out. What she was telling this widow, she later admitted, she was really also telling herself.

Ponder and Pray

- Do you visit cemeteries or avoid them at all costs? Is there a reason for this?

- How was the cemetery shown to be a continuation of life for the Sacred Heart family?

- What symbol or words would you like on your headstone?

Let us pray A Prayer for the Poor Souls in Purgatory

V. Eternal rest grant unto them, O Lord.

R. And let the perpetual light shine upon them.

And may the souls of all the faithful departed, through the mercy of God, rest in peace. Amen.

V. Requiem aeternam dona eis, Domine.

R. Et lux perpetua luceat eis.

Fidelium animae, per misericordiam Dei, requiescant in pace. Amen.

Heart of Jesus, enriching all who invoke Thee, have mercy on us.

"The Resurrection of Christ"
Giovanni Bellini

"Christ Walks on Water"
Ivan Aivazovsky

The Lesson of
The Sand Dollar

"Therefore every loyal person should pray to you in time of distress. Though flood waters threaten, they will never reach him. You are my shelter; you guard me from distress; with joyful shouts of deliverance you surround me." –Psalm 32:6-7

"Jesus Appears on the Shore of Lake Tiberias"
James Tissot

Breakable

You,
The sand dollar I have found,
You are marred with little holes
In your personality,
Powdered and breakable.
I feel your beauty
As I trace the patterns of your face,
And hold you from the salty breath of beachcombers.

You have been picked up many times
But never kept.
There is a void in your center,
Where you carry the memory of your source,
Where you vaguely remember the water
Running through your body.
You wait for me to drop you where I found you—
I shake away your gritty sediment
And see the strength as you emerge from the ocean
And carry the journey on your face.

The legend of the Sand Dollar goes that its beautiful shell tells the story of Jesus. His wounds are recalled on the Sand Dollar in the four nail-like holes where his hands and feet would be; the fifth wound made by the Roman spear is there as well. On one side is etched the shape of an Easter lily with a star in its center, representing the Bethlehem star followed by the wise men. On the reverse is the outline of a Christmas poinsettia. If the Sand Dollar is broken, their teeth, closely resembling five white "doves" emerge. The sand dollar is a symbol of wounds and redemption.

Nanabelle's favorite poem spoke to this theme of beautiful resilience in the face of brokenness. It was "A Psalm of Life" by Henry Wadsworth Longfellow. She'd memorized it in school as a young girl, and it became words she would live by. Interestingly, the subtitle of that poem is "What the Heart of the Young Man Said to the Psalmist." The poem proclaims: "Life is real! Life is earnest! And the grave is not its goal; Dust thou art, to dust returnest, Was not spoken of the soul. Not enjoyment, and not sorrow, Is our destined end or way; But to act, that each tomorrow Find us farther than today."

Just weeks after Grandpapa's death, the Pastor approached Nanabelle and asked her to start a Bereavement Group. "People are hurting in a way that you understand firsthand now. I believe you can really help them." He offered a classroom in the Parish Center to have her meetings. "I'd like it at home," she said. And so it was. It was not surprising that Nanabelle agreed. She was a strong believer in the idea that the more one is hurting, the more one should reach out and help others as an antidote.

One Saturday, after waking up in our own home, my mother suggested we go out to breakfast. She said afterwards she would like to drop in on Nanabelle's Bereavement Group and thank them for their prayers for us, and assure them of our continued prayers for them. We ate a hearty breakfast and then headed to the Red House. As we walked in, we saw a large group and they were sharing their most recent stories of loss. They welcomed my mother's gratitude and prayers. Through tears and even some laughter, all of their stories resounded within the heartbeat of the Red House, so I knew all would be well. It was as though the very house was ministering to them within its walls, as they draped in its chairs and listened to the ticking clocks, drank from the blue willow teacups and ate my grandmother's food. Their stories would become braided into the legacy of what made that house so special. One story in particular stands out, the story of Mrs. L.

Mrs. L. was a convert from Protestantism. Her ancestors had come over on the Mayflower. More recent generations of her family had built a church in our area. A close relative of hers had even been pastor of that church. Yet Mrs. L. had, as she put it, "fallen in love with the one, holy, Catholic and Apostolic Church."

They prayed and discussed Scripture as part of their time together and after reading that Jesus gave Simon his new name, "Peter," and told him, "Upon this rock I will build my church," Mrs. L. said, "And that's the church for me! The true one, built by Jesus on rock, and not splintered off." Mrs. L went on to recount how her family said she had turned her back on them by converting; but she felt like the one who had been left behind.

As I listened, riveted, I thought of the words of Matthew 7:24-25: *"Therefore everyone who hears these words of Mine and acts on them is like a wise man who built his house on the rock. The rain fell, the torrents raged, and the winds blew and beat against that house; yet it did not fall, because its foundation was on the rock. But everyone who hears these words of Mine and does not act on them is like a foolish man who built his house on sand."*

Some years later, Nanabelle and I were having tea in her kitchen when she told me that Mrs. L. had fallen ill and died. "Do you remember Mrs. L?" Nanabelle asked. "Oh, I could never forget her story," I said, "I'm so sorry to hear that she died."

As I listened in wonder, Nanabelle told me how Mrs. L. had called her on the phone just two days before she died. "I'm frightened," she admitted. "All my faith is being tested. I'm scared to think of going in the ground."

"Oh you won't be there," Nanabelle said. "Your soul will be in God's care; not in the ground. Remember what Jesus told the Good Thief? '*On this day you shall be with me in Paradise*' (Lk 23:43). You just hold onto those words of Our Lord. And you just keep praying, 'Jesus, remember me, when you come into your Kingdom.'"

Nanabelle got a call soon after that day from Mrs. L's family, telling her that Mrs. L. died peacefully, thanks to her steady contemplation of Christ's promise to the Good Thief and her constant repeated prayer requesting remembrance by the King. The feud about her conversion to Catholicism was no more. "It was beautiful to see how her faith got her through her last months," they told Nanabelle, "and how your wisdom got her through her final days. Thank you so much for your prayers... and for everything you did for her."

At this point in her telling of the story, Nanabelle paused and went into the Living Room and came back with a beautiful blue and white candlestick with little windmills painted on it. "This is real Delft," Nanabelle said, "antique; it's a treasure from Mrs. L's ancestors. Her family gave it to me after she died. It held a lit candle during her last hours. They gave it to me because they said I had brought her... and all of them... peace."

Many years later, Nanabelle and I were chatting on the phone and reminisced about Mrs. L. once more. I started recounting what I remembered of the story and Nanabelle added, "She was a wonderful and courageous woman who loved her family dearly, but had to follow where faith led her. What a story she had."

"It's your story, too," I answered. "You'd brought her light in the darkness."

The next week when Nanabelle came over my house, she brought me the candlestick. "I know you won't forget her story... you'll keep it in your heart, and you'll share it with others."

In my home, the candlestick is in a place of honor as a reminder to me of everything Nanabelle taught: the light of faith passed to others with Heaven as the goal.

All the people my grandmother helped through tough times, like Mrs. L, and certainly like myself... were like Sand Dollars on a shore: bearing wounds, being swept, and pulled in and out of the tide; washed, reshaped and pushed onto the coarse sand. Nanabelle walked along the shoreline, gathered the Sand Dollars into her basket, and brought us home.

Ponder and Pray

- Are you a member of or facilitator of a faith group? How does it benefit you and others?

- Have you lost family members or friends because you followed your convictions in faith?

- As described in the poem, "The Sand Dollar," when were you like the sand dollar? Explain.

- Who have you rescued? Who have you healed in some unique way or seek to heal? Explain.

Let us pray: Most holy Heart of Jesus, fountain of every blessing, I love You. With a lively sorrow for my sins I offer You this poor heart of mine. Make me humble, patient, and pure, and perfectly obedient to Your Will.

Good Jesus, grant that I may live in You and for You. Protect me in the midst of danger and comfort me in my afflictions. Bestow on me health of body, assistance in temporal needs, Your blessing on all that I do, and the grace of a holy death. Within your heart I place my every care. In every need let me come to you with humble trust saying, Heart of Jesus, help me. Amen.

Heart of Jesus, fountain of light and holiness, have mercy on us.

"Last Supper"
Valentin de Boulogne

The Lesson of The Statue

"Take to heart these words which I command you today. Keep repeating them to your children. Recite them when you are at home and when you are away, when you lie down and when you get up. Bind them on your arm as a sign and let them be as a pendant on your forehead. Write them on the doorposts of your houses and on your gates."
–Deut 6: 6-9

"You shall love the Lord your God, with all your heart, with all your being, with all your strength, and with all your mind, and your neighbor as yourself." –Lk 10:27

"Saint John the Beloved and the Sacred Heart of Jesus" (detail)
Giotto – Scrovegni Chapel

In Praise of the Sacred Heart

"Within His Holy Wounds we fain would hide."
And now, we sing his Sacred Heart, the flame
atop of it that has intensified
with love— the fire that knows us each by name.
We sing the cross atop the heart, each thorn
encircling it like a saving chain,
and binding us to him. Now we adorn
his heart with prayer. We celebrate its reign—
align our clock-like pulse to know his beat.
The ones who mocked him didn't know his heart,
or that he could turn rot to something sweet;
they didn't know he had mastered the art—
that out of pain, he'd make a royal ring.
They didn't know that they had crowned a king.

My mother was born on the Feast of St. John the Beloved Apostle, December 27th. I have come to see the paramount importance of that saint, and how he was the only male follower of Jesus to stand loyally at the foot of the cross and be with Christ throughout his Passion. He had reclined with his head on Jesus' heart during the Last Supper. Having rested on the Sacred Heart, he listened to the secrets therein, and was strengthened for what was to come, bonded to Jesus in a way that made it unthinkable for him to abandon him. The image of St. John at rest on the breast of Jesus is an image for any faithful disciple, leaning upon the strength and unquenchable love found therein as one declares, "Jesus, I trust in you." My mother grew up in my grandmother's Red House as the middle child, and fittingly, was always drawn to the heart of things. She attuned a listening ear to the heart of that home, and in this spirit of love, grew closer to the heart of Jesus and was able to teach it to others. Interestingly, Luke Chapter 12 verse 27 reads this: *Notice how the flowers grow. They do not toil or spin. But I tell you, not even Solomon in all his splendour was dressed like one of them.* Therefore, we are reminded to trust in God. This passage ends, *"For where your treasure is, there also will your heart be."* My mother always treasured "home," that state of being cozy and together in a place of her loving design. She was good at making home a place everyone looked forward to entering. She had memorized the lessons of the Red House she'd grown up in, pondered them in her heart, and trusted in that treasure, enabling her to impart the richness of faith to her students.

One of my mother's earliest memories was one that, although she didn't know it at the time, foreshadowed her future as a much-beloved Catholic educator, passionate catechist and brilliant theology teacher of the youth. The story goes that when she was just a girl of seven, the age for First Holy Communion in her school, something overtook her. She became consumed with all the preparations that the Sacrament required. She saw herself as a true bride of Christ with her white dress and veil, pocketbook with the Children's Missal within, and white gloves to the wrist. She sang the song her class was learning all through the Red House: "Jesus, My Lord, My God, My All." She was so zealous about her first communion that she took her enthusiasm to the atheist neighbors and attempted to convert their young daughter to Catholicism, right down to the wafers for practicing receiving the Body and Blood of Christ. They played Communion joyfully every Saturday and sang "Jesus, My Lord, My God, My All" as they rode on the swings. A phone call from her friend's dad brought the Communion game to a screeching halt, as Nanabelle explained the nuances and challenges of evangelization to her pious young daughter.

My father was born on October 27th, the Vigil of the Feast of Sts. Simon and Jude. St. Jude, author of an epistle in the New Testament, was Jesus's cousin on St. Joseph's side. During the Last Supper discourse, after Jesus said: *"He that loveth Me shall be loved of My Father: and I will love him and will manifest Myself to him,"* Then Jude asked Him: *"Lord, how is it, that Thou wilt manifest Thyself to us, and not to the world?"* He received from Jesus this reply: *"If any one love Me, he will keep My word, and My Father will love him, and We will come to him, and will make Our abode with him. He that loveth Me not keepeth not My word. And the word which you have heard is not Mine, but the Father's who sent Me."* St. Jude is often depicted holding a coin upon which is the Holy Face of Jesus. St. Jude carried a cloth with the Holy Face of Jesus to the King of Edessa and cured him of leprosy. So St. Jude is the apostle of the Holy Face and is also an apostle who learned a lesson of love from Jesus.

My parents, then, were each born on the twenty-seventh of a month, and in both cases their birthdays were associated with apostles devoted to the love of Christ. My mother, in her widowhood, missing my dad, created a beautiful way to honor his memory while teaching her students to love God.

When my mother taught fourth grade, she initiated a day of celebrating our Love of God. Over time, the entire school celebrated this lesson-turned-holiday. Every year on October 27th, they would mark the day with red balloons and a prayer service reminding the school community of these words of Jesus: "to love the Lord your God with your whole heart, whole being, whole strength, whole mind, and your neighbor as yourself." It became known as "The Law of Love Day": Luke 10:27, the twenty-seventh of October, the day their widowed teacher's husband had been born. How many lessons they learned: how to love in a way that endures: to love our God and to love those dear to us.

When she began to teach the upper grade Theology classes, those students she had taught in the fourth grade were her students once more. She sent them out to all the classes in the other grade levels to teach the Law of Love. They enjoyed their mission.

My mother kept my father's memory alive for new generations of students while giving greater glory to God.

Years later, after thirty years of teaching at that same Catholic school, upon her retirement, the school placed a statue of the Sacred Heart of Jesus in a grotto on the school grounds in her honor, along with a plaque stating that my mother taught many students to love Jesus through the annual Law of Love tradition. The Sacred Heart of Jesus points to his heart, just as my mother's teachings always did. Now, her grandchildren stop at that statue to pray after Mass every weekend in the church next to the school, and they are shown the heart of Jesus, and without words, invited to embrace, and listen.

Ponder and Pray

- What statues are in your home or garden?

- Who is the patron saint of your vocation?

- What saint is associated with your name or birthday? Do you have a devotion to them?

- What Scripture passage would you most like to teach to the next generation?

Let us Pray: Sacred Heart of Jesus, I Commit This Day to You: Merciful Heart of Jesus, today, in return for Your great love for me, I renew the covenant of love I made with You on the day of my Baptism and which You renew each time You offer Yourself to the Father in the Eucharist. I consecrate myself, family, and all my undertakings to Your loving Heart. I offer to bring the message of love and mercy that emanates from Your Sacred Heart to all who will listen. Send forth Your Holy Spirit and You shall renew the face of the earth! I ask this through the Immaculate Heart of Mary, Your Mother.

Heart of Jesus, propitiation for our sins, have mercy on us.

"The Sacred Heart of Jesus"
French School

"The Annunciation"
Nicolas Poussin

The Lesson of The Dove

I said, "Oh, that I had wings like a dove! I would fly away and be at rest." –Psalm 55:6

The Golden Chapel of the Sacred Heart

Six healings, carved in wood, sealed in gold leaf,
of paralytics; blind men; deaf and dead;
surround the Sacred Heart statue, relief—
of mercy. As I pray, above my head,
the Savior points to His heart, set aflame,
a Trinity of fingers raised. His eyes
are lowered— for He knows each person's name,
and broken heart, and waits, for He is wise.
The floor is hard and cold, but I am home.
There in the chapel silence with my Lord,
before its reredos, under its dome—
my blindness, deafness, deadness dies. Restored,
I leave, enter the traffic, crowds, fresh air—
longing to run back to my golden prayer.

As I look back, there is a recurring theme of the Sacred Heart in my life. I remember being drawn to the image as a child, moved and amazed by how Jesus literally exposes his heart to us, holding nothing back. One of the most profound moments of my spiritual life came in college while I was keeping watch during my slot for Eucharistic Adoration at chapel, and I felt the true presence of the Sacred Heart of Jesus. Then, as a young college student who had achieved my first international publication, I went to the bookstore to purchase a book I could use to record where I was sending my poems: the date, venue and poems sent. I chose a red leather book, made in Florence, inlaid with an image of the Sacred Heart aflame. I figured that this was one way to be sure my work would be guided by and offered to God. Years later, in my twenties, I took an overnight retreat at the Seminary of the Immaculate Conception, and it was particularly moving. When the retreat ended, I packed my car but did not yet venture home.

Instead, I went down to the Crypt Chapel and entered a side altar of the Sacred Heart, a little chapel within the chapel. I knelt before a gold statue of the Sacred Heart which was beautifully set into golden reredos with scenes from the many healings of Jesus. There was Matthew 9:1-8 "Jesus Forgives and Heals a Paralytic"; Matthew 9:23-26 "Jesus Raises a Dead Girl"; Matthew 9:27-30 "Jesus Heals the Blind and Mute"; Mark 7:32-36 "Jesus Heals a Deaf and Mute Man"; Luke 17:12-14 "Jesus Heals Ten Men With Leprosy"; and John 5:2-9 "Jesus Heals the Man at the Pool of Bethesda".

I thought of the ways I needed healing. I prayed there for a long time, and felt so blissfully happy, that I didn't want to leave. I knew it was Sunday afternoon, and the time had come for me to go back home and get ready for work the next day... but I just wanted to stay there.

I left and drove home reluctantly. And what did I do once there? Well, it was a warm spring day, so after I got a few chores done, I walked across the back lawn and reclined on a deck chair, my eyes closing in the light of the sun. I began to miss the Sacred Heart chapel and the monastic peace that a retreat brings: days dedicated to prayer alone. And after some time, I heard the rustle of feathers and felt something land upon my foot. It was a dove. It sat there a few calm moments, looking at me as I opened my eyes. Then it flapped its wings and flew away. "Thank you, Lord," I prayed.

I'll never forget the feel of that gentle creature perching on my foot, or the sound of the rush of its wings, and how calm I remained through it all. The dove had brought me strength and peace. It was a Sunday, and I'd had my humble Pentecost.

Ponder and Pray

- Was there ever a time you felt so close to the presence of God, that you didn't want to leave?
- Did you ever feel so close to God that you were afraid to stay?
- Think of a time in your life when you thought the Spirit was at work in you. Any visible signs?

Let us pray: Come, Holy Spirit, fill the hearts of your faithful. And kindle in them the fire of your love. Send forth your Spirit and they shall be created. And you will renew the face of the earth. Lord, by the light of the Holy Spirit you have taught the hearts of your faithful. In the same Spirit, help us to relish what is right and always rejoice in your consolation. We ask this through Christ our Lord.

Amen.

Heart of Jesus, loaded down with reproaches, have mercy on us.

"Dove (Holy Spirit) as part of the Holy Trinity"
Johann Michael Rottmayr

The Golden Chapel of the Sacred Heart

A Sonnet Crown to the Sacred Heart as Healer

I

Six healings, carved in wood, sealed in gold leaf,
of paralytics; blind men; deaf and dead;
surround the Sacred Heart statue, relief—
of mercy. As I pray, above my head,
the Savior points to His heart, set aflame,
a Trinity of fingers raised. His eyes
are lowered— for He knows each person's name,
and broken heart, and waits, for He is wise,
The floor is hard and cold, but I am home.
there in the chapel silence with my Lord.
Before its reredos, under its dome,
my blindness, deafness, deadness dies. Restored,
I leave, enter the traffic, crowds, fresh air—
longing to run back to my golden prayer.

Mt 9:1-8

II

Longing to run back to my golden prayer,
I think of the first panel: Matthew Nine—
the Paralytic, healed from his nightmare
of motionlessness, took his mat— walked fine,
and with his sins forgiven, felt a weight
had left him as he rose. How many times
we're paralyzed by sin; it chokes our gait
as though thorn bushes trespass on our climbs.
How many times we're frozen, numb with pain
and when we're told, "your sins are forgiven"
after Confession, it's like light through rain
as we walk out, relieved we were driven
to stop the old familiar ache, confess—
pick up our stretchers, rise— released and blessed.

Mt 9:23-26

III

Pick up our stretchers. Rise, released and blessed:
that is the way it feels to move again
after we're paralyzed. What if the rest
we face is not limb's numbness, but death's pain?
The Master took the dead little girl's hand
and called it sleep, then guided her awake.
What loss will He not transform, understand,
and resurrect? His Sacred Heart can take
dead skin and make it living flesh. That girl
would ride, like Lazarus, the tide from death—
to life, a second chance, a blinding whirl
of light returned, a rushing tide of breath.
Whatever we have in us that is dead—
know He can make it beautiful instead.

Mt 9:27-30

IV

No. He can make it beautiful instead.
Don't doubt it. He transfigures, rises, heals.
Two blind men followed Him once, and they spread
their arms out, crying, making their appeals.
He asked if they believed, He touched their eyes,
and at His touch, their eyes were opened. Just
imagine their first sight: the greatest prize—
His face: those shining eyes, broad smile. Our trust
in Him will heal our blindness, too. The scales
will fall. We'll blink at all His brightness, like
a child looking east on sunrise trails.
He does not give what we deserve: a strike—
rather, a gentle touch, eyes filled with sight.
It's He who drags the dawn into our night.

Mk 7:32-36

V

It's He who drags the dawn into our night,
opens what has been closed. There was a poor,
deaf man with speech impediments, whose plight
moved Christ. Like He was opening a door,
He brought back sound and clear words to the man
with His command, "*Ephphatha*! Be opened!"
The man asked for Christ's touch: a prayerful plan
that we should emulate, not just cope, and
settle for what is broken. So we ask
for what is closed within us to swing wide,
our ears and tongue to be healed, to unmask
our pretenses, and stop trying to hide.
Ephphatha! That comes back to me in prayer—
thinking of His heart, golden as a flare.

Lk 17:12-14

VI

Thinking of His heart, golden as a flare
upon the chapel statue, open wide
to priest's incense or pilgrim's trembling prayer,
imagine ten lepers, freed of their pride
all calling out: Have pity! Only one
returned. Let us pray: let that one be me,
saved by faith, drawn by gratitude to run.
Let's be as loud with our thanks, as our plea.
In fair Bethesda were five porticoes
at the Sheep Gate Pool, where an ill man lay.
Old and frail, his skin was corticose.
Three decades there; it seemed he'd rather stay,
complaining than be healed, but Christ said, Rise!
Like stirred water, Love came as a surprise.

Jn 5:2-9

VII

Like stirred water, Love came as a surprise
inside the gold chapel, under its dome.
Restored— my blindness, deafness, deadness dies.
There with the Sacred Heart, there I am home—
the chapel's where I trust, let go of shame,
and give my heart. He waits there with His wise
gaze lowered—for He knows each person's name,
his Trinity of fingers, raised. Those eyes!
The Savior points to His heart: burning grief,
love, mercy. As I pray, above my head,
around the Sacred Heart statue, relief—
of paralytics; blind men; deaf and dead;
all these who were made new through grace, belief—
Six healings, carved in wood, sealed in gold leaf.

"Still Life with Open Bible, Candlestick, and Novel"
Vincent van Gogh

The Lesson of
The Book

"What woman having ten coins and losing one would not light a lamp and sweep the house searching carefully until she finds it? And when she does find it, she calls together her friends and neighbors and says to them, 'Rejoice with me...'"
—Lk 15:8-9

"Young Girl Reading"
Jean-Honoré Fragonard

Light in August

I haven't heard your voice in twenty-five years—
but this evening, as the amber light of summer's last days
sweetened the coming darkness like ripe honey—
one of your old books was found, behind a shelf in the
basement.

This is the time of year you would have opened it again,
Teacher that you were,
reviewing the themes and metaphors,
ready to discuss Faulkner's outcasts.

It is an eighth-month evening, percussive with crickets.
My eyes leap ahead to the words you underlined:
<u>When she was twelve years old her father and mother died</u>
—and you didn't know I would lose you at eleven.

The story I still need all these years later is the one you've
started—
just with the words you circled, Daddy, the sight of your
singular penmanship—
the exclamation mark pencilled near a phrase you liked,
garland of Augusttremulous lights.

The *garland of Augusttremulous lights* you left for me:
carefully chosen words rising up like fireflies or bonfire sparks,
a confirmation—
singeing this vigil of study, reminding of all I've never been
able to ask you—
and teaching me, through the wise words you chose to mark—

I'd never have reached the end of all I could learn from you.

One day in August, a book was found, in the recesses of the basement of my childhood home. It was my father's. It had so many of his under-linings in it, and even some notes written in his own hand. The blue hardback was Faulkner's *Light in August*. It was amazing that it had been uncovered in the month of August. Recalling that he had taught that book to his high school students, I quickly realized this discovery was like a Rosetta Stone revealing more than just itself, but his teaching style and insight into his soul. There were questions he had written on the sides to ask his students, vocabulary words on which to test them, and exclamations marked near anything he found moving. This affected me deeply because I myself had become a teacher. Through the notes left behind in his book, it was almost as though I could speak with him, as one teacher to another.

After college and graduate school, I taught English at a Catholic high school and proudly hung the very same portrait of William Shakespeare that had been prominently displayed in my father's classroom, now in my own. I'd catch a glimpse of that picture now and then as I taught and just for a moment would remember being a little girl helping my father decorate his classroom every August. There were more than a few occasions that I would speak at Meet the Teacher night and a parent of one of my students would approach me and tell me that my father had been *their* teacher. They always told me how much they had learned from him, how much he had encouraged them to reach their fullest potential, and how he saw gifts in them that they themselves had not. I worked to be the kind of teacher he was, and after four years when I left my high school teaching job to become a college and Graduate School Theology professor, I vowed to continue that same spirit of excitement for the subject and dedication to my students as I had learned from my dad.

With my *Light in August* discovery, it was clear how much work he put into those he taught and it was like having a conversation with him again after twenty-five years. He was teaching me once more.

Ponder and Pray

- Do you ever underline in books? Why or why not?

- Do you ever go back to the under-linings in your book or Bible; or a loved one's book? Does it bring comfort or insight? Why? What thoughts and feelings does it evoke?

- How is finding the under-linings and jotted notes in a loved ones book akin to finding a gold-mine?

- Have you ever found a long-forgotten or hidden, misplaced or lost object that brought back a wealth of memories or a connection to a particular person or place that was important in your life?

Let us pray The Golden Arrow (as dictated by Our Lord to Sister Marie of St. Peter):

May the most holy, most sacred, most adorable, most incomprehensible and ineffable Name of God be forever praised, blessed, loved, adored and glorified in Heaven, on Earth, and under the Earth by all the creatures of God and by the Sacred Heart of Our Lord Jesus Christ in the Most Holy Sacrament of the Altar. Amen. Eternal Father, I offer Thee the adorable Face of Thy Beloved Son for the honour and glory of Thy Name, for the conversion of sinners and the salvation of the dying.

Amen

Admirable is the name of God!

Amen.

Heart of Jesus, bruised for our offences, have mercy on us.

"Still Life with Books and Candle"
Henri Matisse

"Madonna del velo"
Ambrogio Bergognone

The Lesson of The Birth Offering

"Let my prayer be incense before you; my uplifted hands an evening offering."
Psalm 131:2

"No. 17 Scenes from the Life of Christ: 1. Nativity" (detail)
Giotto di Bondone

The Nativity

"She gave birth," Scripture says. One line to tell
of Mary's sacrifice. A mother knows
how much that means—the way each tiny cell
within each muscle feels a labor's throes.
And yet a mother wills the searing pain.
Her suffering allows her dear one birth.
And through a mother's long, heroic strain,
she focuses upon the gift's great worth.
Mary's libation, offered up to God
presented love through body, soul, and will.
She felt him near, she almost felt him nod.
For through Christ's passion, God's Word would fulfill—
through water and through blood, deliver all
to life—pushing through Calvary's grim caul.

My grandmother would remind me each time I was expecting and when my time was drawing near of what Fr. T., her brother, told her right before she gave birth to each of her six children: "No one is closer to God than a woman in labor." My grandmother lived to the age of 101, and even in her last days, she still loved to recall her brother and spiritual advisor strengthening her with this reminder.

When Fr. T. finally returned to America after the war, malnourished and suffering from the malaria he'd contracted in the prison camp, he found my grandmother close to her delivery date. "Please pray for me while you're in labor," he humbly asked, "that God will strengthen me."

From that point on, my grandmother always brought special intentions with her when she went into labor, and she taught me to do the same. Praying for others while giving birth is a wonderful way to focus one's breathing and keep one's soul focused and aware of the sacredness of the moment. With my first labor, it felt like a privilege to offer up the pain I experienced for special intentions just the way I had always heard my grandmother had. I also learned what I would experience with each of my labors: that I have never felt closer to the communion of saints.

It is a rare moment, as one labors with the Creator to birth a new life, that the veil between Heaven and earth feels much thinner and our saints, our great cloud of witnesses, have never seemed closer to me.

As two souls and bodies prepared to separate and bond in a new way, it was indeed a well-appointed time to ask for special blessings for my soon-to-be-born little one and for the love we would share, as well as to ask for the strength my husband and I would need to parent that child. Besides praying for my child and soon-to-be expanded family, I placed before God the special intentions I'd chosen to bring with me.

While my husband was driving me to the hospital to give birth to my second baby, my phone rang. It was my grandmother calling. "Hello, my dear, are you on your way to the hospital, by any chance?" I hadn't had the chance to tell anyone this yet and wondered how she could have known. "Yes I am!" I exclaimed, as we were that very moment pulling into the hospital parking lot. "I just knew it," she said. "I've been praying for you and I could feel that your time had come. Well, you know what to do," she reminded, "Just like last time. Pray for others. Offer everything up. And I'll be praying for you."

Ponder and Pray

- All births tell a unique story. Do you have an interesting birth story that you can share? Where do you see God's hand in your birth or life?

- Look up your date of birth and discover, if you don't already know, which saint's feast day shares your birthday. Invoke this saint in prayer. Look up the details of this saint's life. How is this feast day or saint's day fitting for your birthday? Is there some patronage or element of the saint that you resonate with or some part of the saint's life you wish to strive to emulate?

- Have you consecrated yourself and/or your children to the Sacred Heart of Jesus and the Immaculate Heart of Mary? Would you consider doing so now?

Let us pray: the Prayer to the Sacred Heart of Jesus, from Rafael Cardinal Merry de Val

Jesus, reveal Your Sacred Heart to me and show me Its attractions. Unite me to It forever. Grant that all my desires and every beat of my heart, which does not cease even while I sleep, may be a witness to You of my love for You and tell You: Yes Lord, I am Yours! The pledge of my loyalty to You rests ever in my heart and shall never cease to be there. Accept the little good that I do and be pleased to make up for all my wrong-doing so that I may be able to praise You in time and in eternity.

Amen.

Heart of Jesus, obedient unto death, have mercy on us.

"Adoration of the Christ Child"
Gerard van Honthorst

"Annunciation with St. Emidius"
Carlo Crivelli

The Lesson of
The Peacock Pin

"Wherever you go I will go, wherever you lodge I will lodge. Your people shall be my people and your God, my God." –Ruth 1:16

"Adoration of the Magi"
Fra Angelico

You Should Know

I

First of all, your beauty has lasted and ripened
through everything you've suffered.
And like the plumes of the peacock,
your startling beauty is full of eyes—
watchful eyes that have journeyed a pilgrimage,
peacock-blue eyes unblinking in the wind,
staring down the storm, your eyes
have made ours open wider.

II

In case you've forgotten—
when my father lay dying,
you took the child I was to the hospital gift shop
and bought me the pin I liked.
I still have it—
an enamel peacock,
sitting on a branch.
Why would I reach for that elegant bird
at such a sparse time?
Something about the contrast maybe.
Or my subconscious recognized the covenant shape
of a bird holding a branch,
hope in the deluge.

III

Every year, peacocks shed old feathers
and grow new, brighter ones.
And so, the Roman catacombs are filled
with paintings of that bird of renewal,
and came to symbolize Christ.
Down in the dark

in the hidden places
where air meets root,
faith was tested and sheltered,
the peacock strutted a bold resurrection.

IV

When you leave us,
we'll work to raise our tremolos in song,
to transform knee-sore anguish into prayer.
This, because we know
your feather-shaped soul will jubilate,
as it joins the great wing of saints.
You running, riding the tide of
an ocean we have never swum,
all the while we are bound by gravity.

V

The peacock pin's long, thin, gold tooth is sharp.
Its point hurts the flesh—
reminds how your body has suffered,
how our family's body will bleed when you go.
But—
it reminds that there will be a fastening.
Yes, you should know how it is with us,
how it is between you and us.
There will be a fastening.
I say it again. I shout it. I swear it.
We pin you to us.
Do you hear?
Even as you go, and I mean really travel well,
We pin you to us.
We pin your beauty,
we pin your sorrowful and glorious mysteries,
We pin you
to the unfinished saints you leave behind.

The Peacock Pin

M ay we always have as much," Nanabelle said each Thanksgiving, at the close of Grace. The Thanksgiving table had to be stretched to capacity, with so many of us crowding about. There is a Hebrew word for family, *Mishpacha*, that a Jewish friend once told me is meant to suggest a vast group, the whole clan, as it were. It includes in-laws, second and third cousins, and can even include close friends who are braided into the family story. In my grandmother's house, there were many visitors; not only her eight living siblings and their families, her own six children, twelve grandchildren and four great-grandchildren, but also friends and neighbors. She made all feel at home. The ancient Jewish tradition of hospitality that shone in such figures as Abraham and Sarah, and was apparent in Mary's concern for the Cana wine and Jesus's humble and loving washing of his friends' feet, was alive and well in the House of the Sacred Heart.

And so, I daresay, the in-laws that had married into our family were treasured. They were made to feel welcome and their gifts and strengths were pinned to ours. I grew up surrounded by jewelry pins. The women in my family loved to wear them. Bright, sparkling jewels crested sweaters and jackets. When each new baby was dressed for their Baptism, a Blessed Mother medal was pinned to them. And I think that my family's reverence for our beloved dead: our staunch tradition of praying for them and telling stories of their lives was another kind of pin. I came to see that in my family, we pinned what was important to the family tapestry.

When my father was in the hospital, my aunt, Uncle E's wife, stopped by and offered to take me for a walk through the hospital to stretch my legs.

"Annabelle, why don't we go check out the gift shop?" Aunt L suggested, her blue eyes widening as she smiled.

I complied more out of not wanting to hurt her feelings than out of any desire to go. We didn't speak much as we walked, but I was aware of how badly she felt; how much she wanted to comfort me. She was good at hospitals, my aunt. She had a certain ministry when it came to visiting the sick and the sad and cheering them up. I'd call it her apostolate.

In the gift shop, she showed me some colored silk scarves that she thought were pretty, asked me which one I liked. There was a fringed sea green scarf, a lovely color, but I just shrugged. Its beauty and softness seemed frivolous to me somehow in the midst of such darkness. Then my aunt asked if I would like a lollipop or some fudge.

"No, thanks; I'm okay," I said, knowing I couldn't have eaten a bite.

But then my eye caught something in the jewelry case in front of the counter. It was a red peacock brooch with a golden tail. The head was turned to the side and looked at me with one small round eye.

"I like that," I said with a weak smile. I had finally caught on that my aunt was hoping to buy me something. Fortunately, it was not too expensive. Before I knew it, she had purchased it and was pinning it on me.

"There, now," she said, "That looks nice."

In the medieval era, because of a legend that its flesh did not decay, peacocks were thought to represent resurrection and immortality. I knew nothing of that symbol as I instinctively reached for it, as I pointed to the pinned thing in the glass case, as it was taken out of its holder and attached to my sweater. I would wear it almost every day that I went to the hospital, perched on my shoulder, looking at the world from its one eye, right above my heart.

What a meaningful gift that was for her to give a child: something beautiful that contrasted the grayness through which I was living.

Years later, when my Aunt L was dying, and I learned she had only days to live, I wanted so much to give her something; to be of some use to her. I fastened the peacock pin to me, and out poured a poem to her, in which I promised her "We pin you to us."

Reading that to her as she listened was difficult but also rewarding. She smiled, knowing she could take those words with her on the journey, and she asked for the poem to be shown at her wake.

Her death hit the family hard, much as my father's death had. Nanabelle, my mother's siblings and the rest claimed their in-laws as "brother" and "sister" not only at celebrations like Thanksgiving when we all counted our blessings, but in the way we mourned their deaths. I still remember my aunts and uncles designing a bouquet to be sent to my father's wake and insisting to the florist, "No, not 'Beloved Brother-in-Law'. We want the sign to say 'Beloved Brother.' He was our brother." They did the same for my aunt, referring to her as 'Sister.'

The peacock pin has represented to me the way we join all our family members into our story.

We pin our loved ones to us. They are part of us, fastened to us, and the threads of our story are stitched with theirs. God allows us, through marriage, to bring new people into our stories and we all have learned much from those who joined our families. We are blessed. In the words of Nanabelle, "May we always have as much."

Ponder and Pray

- What loved one(s) do you feel "forever pinned" to and why?
- Who do you think might pin themselves to you by your example of love and faith?

Let us pray the Evening Prayer Collect for the Feast of the Most Sacred Heart of Jesus

O God, who in the Heart of your Son, wounded by our sins, bestow on us in mercy the boundless treasures of your love, grant, we pray, that, in paying him the homage of our devotion, we may also offer worthy reparation. Through our Lord Jesus Christ, your Son, who lives and reigns with you in the unity of the Holy Spirit, one God, for ever and ever.

May the Lord bless us, protect us from all evil and bring us to everlasting life. Amen.

Heart of Jesus, pierced with a lance, have mercy on us.

"Transfiguration"
Titian

The Lesson of The Elevator

"After six days Jesus took with him Peter, James and John the brother of James, and led them up a high mountain by themselves. There he was transfigured before them. His face shone like the sun, and his clothes became as white as the light."
—Mt 17:1-2

"The Transfiguration"
Giovanni Bellini

On The Feast of the Transfiguration

(for A.B.)

We are your seven witnesses
upon this mountain, just outside the O.R.,

followed as they wheeled you down the hall,
crowded in the elevator as it rose—

We gather around your hospital bed
like a half-crown of stars.

Then, just before your operation begins,
you lead us in the *Anima Christi*.

For a moment, the nurses pause their preparations;
the doctor lowers his head. Residents stop their chatter.

Soon, there will be three pins in your fractured hip
and a cast on your broken wrist.

Your one hundred year old body
will struggle to walk again, to lift spoon to mouth.

But, the Body of Christ, with outstretched arms
will guard each step you take, with parent-pride

And as you falter and feel pain, even as you sleep,
know this: you have transfigured us.

In early August 2017, Nanabelle took a bad fall, fracturing her hip and breaking her shoulder. It was doubted whether she would even make it through surgery. When I joined several other family members at the hospital, and listened to the doctor describe the bleak risks she faced, we felt sick to the core.

By the time we were told, "We are taking Annabelle to the O.R. now. You can all follow," our witty sage had already charmed every nurse on the floor. As she was wheeled toward the elevator, each of them stopped to speak to her, looking like they'd received the best gift as she answered them, and smiled, still so beautiful.

I walked at the very back of the line, watching the bowed, graying heads of my mother, aunts and uncles, the faith-filled children she and Grandpapa had raised— as they followed their mother. I realized today was the Feast of the Transfiguration and that however it ended up, Nanabelle was going to be transfigured and the seven of us were blessed to be there as her witnesses, we who followed her up the mountain, ascending floors to the O.R.

As we all piled into the elevator, her words broke the quiet tension. "Well, this could be fun," she joked, as the elevator ascended. We all laughed through bleary eyes.

When we got just outside the O.R. we gathered around her bed in a semi-circle like a crescent moon, while doctors explained the surgery. We told her of our love, spoke to her of the procedure, shifted nervously. She told us she loved us, too, and that she was proud of how active we were in our church community. It was then that my grandmother said she would like to pray the *Anima Christi* together. Tears fell to the floor as voices melded:

"Soul of Christ, be my sanctification;/ Body of Christ, be my salvation;/ Blood of Christ, fill all my veins;/ Water of Christ's side, wash out my stains,/ Passion of Christ, my comfort be,/ O good Jesus, listen to me/ In Thy wounds I fain would hide/ Ne'er to be parted from Thy side;/ Guard me should the foe assail me;/ Call me when my life shall fail me./ Bid me come to Thee above,/ With Thy Saints to sing Thy love,/ World without end. Amen."

Even the doctors and interns in this public hospital stopped and bowed their heads in prayerful silence as she made this entreaty to Christ her potential goodbye to this world and her certain legacy to us. For the words of the *Anima Christi* she spoke were not only pleas for her own soul. They were the richest inheritance she could bequeath.

On the Feast of the Transfiguration, she made us feel as though our ride up the elevator to the O.R. Had brought us to the peak of a mountain, witnessing a transforming light of assuring grace for this woman of great faith, leading us in prayer in her most frightened hour.

At over one hundred years old, Nanabelle came through the surgery formidably, and proceeded to survive months at two very challenging rehabilitation centers where she faced pain and fear with grace; even in her brokenness. She could barely even lift spoon to mouth unassisted, she had to learn to walk again, but she kept teaching all her children how to follow her, taking trembling steps each day across a stormy but sure path. Despite the frightening sea below her feet, she kept her eyes fixed on Christ. At the end of every visit, she would lead us in the *Anima Christi*. Against all odds, she returned to her home with family in time for the holidays, leading us in that prayer at the Thanksgiving table.

My grandmother proved all along the way that you are never too old, too frail, or too ill to change hearts and inspire souls. On the other side of 100, Annabelle was still looking forward to what Christ has in store for her. Though she used to wonder why He has kept her on this side of Heaven for so long, she now trusts that her earthly work is never over, not even a bit, until the day He calls her home.

We had asked ourselves before what we would do someday without such a presence as my grandmother. Many of us have secretly asked that question about one we love. But through her example we came to realize that though we would someday have to miss her, we would never let our grief blur our duty. We knew we would be close to her always through the Messenger in the Tabernacle, and through the *Anima Christi*, prayed after Eucharist. "Do this in memory of me," Christ beseeched. And, thanks to her passionate teachings of the love of the *Anima Christi*, we had learned how my grandmother would want us to honor her memory: through our adoration and praise of the Body of Christ.

Ponder and Pray

- Have you experienced anything that was like unto a Transfiguration for yourself or your family? Some event that left you changed utterly, for the better, even if difficult?

- Do you think it's possible to ever totally drift away from your faith after experiencing a memorably transfiguring witness to and model of faith?

- One of Nanabelle's favorite go-to prayers was the Anima Christi, a prayer she learned for her first Holy Communion. It became her compass through a lifetime of sorrows and joys. What prayer springs to your lips when words fail you but you need all the help your faith can give?

- The *Anima Christi*, an ancient prayer perfectly suited to being offered after Communion, is attributed to Pope John XXII (1316-1334) but St. Ignatius of Loyola helped popularize it. Nanabelle prayed The Anima Christi many times a day, and always after receiving Eucharist. But not just any version of the Anima Christi, mind you! There are several translations, but she insisted on the one written by Saint John Henry Cardinal Newman in 1913. It's beautiful and effortless rhyme is easy to commit to memory. Do you know the history behind your favorite prayer?

- People love to ask centenarians for advice on "how to live well till 100." Nanabelle said that The Anima Christi is the answer. She advised regular use of this prayer for requesting help and giving praise. She said we can all live by the *Anima Christi*, saying the words after Communion, before sleep, and when facing fear. Through it, we can train our soul to articulate everything we could ever need to ask of Christ, even in times of great trial. How do you train your soul so that you may have good spiritual habits by the time you're a centenarian?

Let us pray the *Anima Christi* (as translated by St. John Henry Cardinal Newman

Soul of Christ, be my sanctification;
Body of Christ, be my salvation;
Blood of Christ, fill all my veins;
Water of Christ's side, wash out my stains;
Passion of Christ, my comfort be;
O good Jesus, listen to me;
In Thy wounds I fain would hide;
Ne'er to be parted from Thy side;
Guard me, should the foe assail me;
Call me when my life shall fail me;
Bid me come to Thee above,
With Thy saints to sing Thy love,
World without end.

Amen.

Heart of Jesus, source of all consolation, have mercy on us.

"The Transfiguration of Christ"
Raphael

"Christ Blessing The Children"
Antoine Ansiaux

The Lesson of The Sage's Blessing

"Now that I am old and gray, do not forsake me, God, that I may proclaim your might to all generations yet to come, your power and justice, God, to the highest heaven." –Psalm 71:18-19

"Resplendent and unfading is Wisdom, and she is readily perceived by those who love her, and found by those who seek her." –Wis 6:12

"The Prophet Anna"
Rembrandt van Rijn

A Prayer for Setting the Table

to Nanabelle, on her 100th Birthday

As the tablecloth unfurls like an altar linen,
as napkins are folded and cups are placed
with the dishes of ordinary time—
I pray for you, to be like you.
It isn't always in words.
Sometimes, the motion of my fingers is the prayer
over the rosary of daily tasks—
smoothing folds of fabric, scraping pots,
polishing kitchen sacramentals.

You know the way the room breathes—
as bowls are taken out and put away?
Of course you know it well—
The daily push of it all.
You've always been one for doing, pursuing—
moving forward.

Yet you are our table and we sit around you.
We pray to nourish others the way you nourish us.
For our tables to welcome, food sustain,
to have enough left for the guests we do not expect—
for our words to anoint like oil.

Here is something I have never told you.
Those many childhood nights I ate at your table,
where life's mysteries were broken and shared—
I studied the blue willow plates
you set each night.
Even during the worst winter, my fork swept potatoes, gravy,
bits of savory meat
and uncovered a story.

Our House of the Sacred Heart

Cast in the familiar pattern,
there were pagodas, fences, shining waterways
and a boat with a figure searching the horizon.
But what kind of wind made the willow fronds splay so far
apart?
Who were the three figures holding lanterns on a bridge?
Each night I told myself a different tale
found hope in the pair of birds, above it all—
larger than the strife below.

You fed me from willow-patterned dishes
when I didn't think I could eat,
when my father was dying
and daffodils were frozen under snow.
But always on your plates
flying above this relentless searching—
two birds, facing each other, wings arched in triumph.
That winter, in blue and white patterns,
the Holy Spirit, in its many-feathered glory
showed itself
on each dish
you placed before me.

This is how you've always fed your family.
Even now, as our tablecloth unfurls like an altar linen,
as napkins are folded and cups are placed
with the dishes of ordinary time—
We pray for you, to be like you.
It isn't always in words.

On Nanabelle's one hundredth birthday, my mother hosted a party in her honor. I gave her a poem I had written for the occasion, entitled, "A Prayer for Setting the Table." As the party was drawing to a close, my grandmother was sitting in a chair in the living room, and I was sitting at her feet. We were alone in the room and I seized the moment. In the spirit of the Old Testament, I looked up at her and asked her this question:

"Since it's your hundredth birthday, on this special day, could I ask you... would you give me your blessing?"

"Oh, yes!" she said without hesitation. I was surprised by how quickly she responded, how she launched into it, lucidly and heartily. She held up her hands and placed them on my bowed head; and I felt like we were a female version of Jacob and Isaac. She said, "God bless you. You're a good girl. Stay as sweet as you are. Amen." Then she explained that those were the exact same words her grandmother gave in blessing every Sunday when Nanabelle and her brother, T., visited after Mass. Their grandmother would ask them to come right to her house after church each week so that she could bring them a cup of water to honor the teaching of Matthew 10:42: "And whosoever shall give to drink to one of these little ones a cup of cold water only in the name of a disciple, amen I say to you, he shall not lose his reward."

Looking back, I realize that my grandmother was one of the best friends I've ever had. We spent so much time together, going shopping, sharing meals, and we had so many of the same interests. Best of all, our personalities melded. She was a force of energy and opinions, and I authentically agreed with everything she said and went happily wherever she led. I was an old soul and she actually enjoyed that. We laughed at the same things, and though we were over sixty years apart in age, saw the world in much the same way. She often told me her childhood ended in many ways when she was ten, because she was needed to care for her mother's ever-expanding family. My childhood ended around the same age, when loved ones passed away. She knew me so well, had watched me grow, and had witnessed the hardest days of my life. When my grandmother died, I felt such pain that she was gone from the world. As our eldest Magnolia, she had truly helped my mother and me each carry our cross. I like to think we helped carry her's, too.

Here's a few pearls of Nanabelle's wisdom; you'll see why I sought her blessing the way others might have sought expensive jewels. Here's 50 Life Lessons from her:

1. Like your own company: "You have to be able to stand yourself," Nanabelle said. There is a lot of talk about learning to "love yourself" but not as much about enjoying being alone and not letting feelings of guilt, insecurity, boredom, or self-doubt spoil your joy.

2. Have a sense of humor: Nanabelle had a sign on the outside of her door that says, "Gone Crazy." She loved to tell funny stories, like the time she got into the wrong car, put all her groceries in it and only then realized it wasn't hers!

3. Realize that humor can be developed and built up over time, like a muscle. It can keep you humble, too! Nanabelle remembered telling her mother with great concern that she had a run in her stocking and her mother answered, "Walk fast and no one will notice."

4. Know what your favorite things are: candy, song, color, teacher, meal, etc. It helps explain who you are: to yourself... and to others.

5. Have your own favorite word: "Hope" is a good one; that was Nanabelle's... or any word that speaks to your soul.

6. Be more interested in loving than in being loved. Along with this, think of other people more than yourself.

7. Have teatime as a daily ritual. Teapot required! There is just something about the pouring of hot water over tea leaves in a bright pot, poured and savored alone or with others that heals the body and soul. Note: black tea with milk and sugar tastes great!

8. Music should be an active part of your life, even better if you make it yourself. Dust off the instrument you played in high school or sing in the shower! When Nanabelle was young, she would often come home to her father playing the piano and her mother singing along. They were not professional musicians but they kept themselves and the family in good cheer by sharing their melodies.

9. Do something daily to keep your brain sharp: Nanabelle read a lot, did crosswords daily and played piano.

10. Memorize poetry. Discover poems that mean the most to you and quote them when needing to find meaning or share wisdom with others. Nanabelle's favorite: "A Psalm of Life" by Longfellow.

11. Walk for exercise. When possible, climb the stairs. Walk and climb the stairs enough and you'll never need a gym membership. As a side note, Nanabelle recommends: if possible, walk to the bakery to get chocolate cake and then come home and eat a piece, guilt-free (bonus points if you do so while the kids are napping)!

12. Appreciate every age group: All have something to celebrate and something to teach.

13. Be grateful. Nanabelle believed in the power of grace before meals, and she always prayed in this way: after the grace before meals adding, "We pray for those who are not as fortunate as we are. And may we always have as much!"

14. Be charitable. Help the needy. Teach the young. Protect the innocent.

15. Look for the simple joys. When life is difficult it can be the little things that get you through: a good book, a bike ride, a bubble bath.

16. Learn to speak up for yourself. As Nanabelle would say, "God gave you a mouth; use it."

17. Don't put money first in your life, or you'll lose your soul.

18. If you are a boss, be the kind of boss you wish you had.

19. Persevere. Have fortitude. Do your best to hang in there when times get tough.

20. Laugh every day: By the way, it's okay to laugh over something silly even in the midst of the darkest times. Laughter keeps you young.

21. Your home should display your faith. People who enter should know who or what you worship. Nanabelle always had religious art on the wall, tastefully displayed, as a clear reminder that her faith was an important part of her life.

22. Having a family is a beautiful and heroic act: so be not afraid! Nanabelle said, "don't be afraid to have children. I had six and it was tough sometimes, I was

overwhelmed at times, but I never regretted one of them. Each of them enhanced my life." Of course she understood it can be intimidating to imagine caring for a completely dependent being, or adding another mouth to feed. But she said raising your kids is the best time of your life, hands down, and she has known the joys of every stage. She would have done it all again, in a heartbeat. Not much sleep, interrupted meals, all plans go out the window—but there is nothing better than life in the making! And with loss of planning and letting go of control, a new kind of freedom follows.

23. Everyone in the family should pitch in. Many hands make light work.

24. Don't be afraid to tell your grown kids what to do sometimes. Overstep a little if you see that their decision could potentially create unhappiness or squander their gifts. They will appreciate your concern and guidance in the long run.

25. Take the time to talk with your children. Discuss their joys and concerns and share your stories. Stories of important people and events in your own life shared with your kids gives a better appreciation of you and a greater sense of identity and belonging.

26. Don't overly brag about your kids. It is ungracious, off-putting and worst of all, could come back to bite you. It can also put too much pressure on the children.

27. Discuss things at the table. Try to keep the custom of having a special Sunday dinner together as a family.

28. Get involved in outreach or charity work. There are so many ministries that need the exact type of gift you can provide and you'd be surprised how much satisfaction

you will reap from your involvement as you make new friends and help others.

29. Have your own favorite go-to prayers. Nanabelle regularly prayed the *Anima Christi* after Communion. She recommended that when you don't know what to pray, just give praise. The Gloria is a great prayer for that.

30. Keep holy the Sabbath. Don't miss Mass, and if you must due to circumstances out of your control, then honor the day in prayer.

31. The best gift you can give your children is to ensure that they know God.

32. All good parents should make sacrifices when it is in their children's best interests. This is especially true when it comes to education and morality. Nanabelle was proud of her and her husband's sacrifice to give all six of their children a Catholic education.

33. Have family traditions. Nanabelle's family always played cards—euchre, at her Aunt Mamie's house while her dad and uncle performed music. Nanabelle's children liked board games and movies shared together with ice cream.

34. Always have extra food ready: you never know when someone will be hungry. Nanabelle vividly recalled the Great Depression. When a man came to the house looking for work, rather than turn him away empty-handed, her mother gave him a plate of meat loaf, stewed tomatoes, and veggies.

35. Comfort food really can comfort. Some of Nanabelle's favorite indulgences included: hot dog and ice cream soda, pot roast and mashed potatoes, a thin slice of pizza with Pepsi free, frozen yogurt, a cup of hot tea with homemade peach pie, cookies, sugar on her cereal and butter on her vegetables...and an occasional cordial glass of Harvey's Bristol Cream Sherry.

36. Keep making friends. Family is everything. It is what it's all about, but Nanabelle's friends have gotten her through a lot. Don't be afraid to keep reaching out.

37. Don't suffer alone. Invite your family, friends and prayer into your heart when things get difficult.

38. Make not-so-pleasant tasks pleasant. When you go out to throw out your garbage or do some other menial task, look around at the flowers or up at the stars.

39. Don't envy. It eats you up from the inside. In a similar way, don't hold on to grudges or anything that gnaws away at your soul and festers. It's not worth it!

40. Shakespeare was right. Especially when it comes to sleep. "Sleep...knits up the raveled sleeve of care." Nanabelle put a lot of store in sleep. Naps for babies and elderly, proper amount of rest for adults.

41. Travel is over-rated. Making a house worth coming home to is more valuable. Besides, the most rewarding journey is the one we navigate within our own soul over a lifetime.

42. Examine your conscience. Each night as you get ready for bed ask yourself: "Where did I go wrong today?" And try to do better tomorrow.

43. Rise and shine. Try to find ways to be joyful and grateful for a new day...every day.

44. There are things to really look forward to about getting old. Here's one: don't be afraid to embody the best qualities of a matriarch or patriarch: setting a strong, wise and loving example for the whole family.

45. Cultivate curiosity and wonder. Be eager to know how the stories continue in the lives of all those you love.

46. Wherever you go in life: bloom where you are planted! When you are old and your living arrangement changes, remember to seek new friends (it's never too late) and find a way to be of help to people.

47. Remember always that we are part of a "communion of saints." There is a bridge connecting loved ones on earth to loved ones in Heaven. Nanabelle looked for signs from her loved ones who had passed. Once you are in the habit, you will find those signs often.

48. Be authentic. When everything else fades away: youth, beauty, money, power, career: what remains is the authentic life you've built and fostered: that is your true legacy.

49. Remember to keep loving yourself, with all your imperfections.

50. Never forget that God loves you. See God in all things. When Nanabelle was a young child, she recalled feeling God's presence loving her for the first time when she pushed a treasured doll carriage in the warm sunlight. Later in life, She said she feels God loving her in all the people He sends her way. What a beautiful arc this

makes: from the light of the sun to the light of loved faces.

Ponder and Pray

- In his 1999 "Letter to the Elderly," Pope Saint John Paul II wrote, "Elderly people help us to see human affairs with greater wisdom, because life's vicissitudes have brought them knowledge and maturity. They are the guardians of our collective memory, and thus the privileged interpreters of that body of ideals and common values which support and guide life in society. Precisely because of their mature experience, the elderly are able to offer young people precious advice and guidance." How do you feel about this quote?

- Nanabelle and Grandpapa both taught how to live and how to serve God, even unto their final breath. What person have you known who has taught you in such a way?

- What sage in your life might you like to ask for a blessing?

Let us pray the Evening Prayer to the Sacred Heart

Heart of Jesus, of whose fullness we have all received, we thank You for Your great goodness to us today. Heart of Jesus, bruised for our offenses, forgive us our sins. Heart of Jesus, most worthy of all praise, may the angels and saints praise You while we are asleep. Dear Saviour, in the tenderness of Your Heart, watch over us tonight and always.

Amen.

Heart of Jesus, our life and resurrection, have mercy on us.

"Jacob Blessing the Children of Joseph"
Rembrandt van Rijn

"Madonna of the Rosary"
Giovanni Battista Paggi

The Lesson of The Child's Blessing

"Jesus said, 'Let the little children come to me, and do not hinder them, for the kingdom of heaven belongs to such as these.'" –Mt 19:14

Hope

A heart hangs like a chrysalis from a branch
in the body's tree-hollow.
Four months before your birth, my child
the doctors worried about your pulse—
resounding inside me.
I wondered what would fly out from your cocoon,
my little one, measured in beats?
What would fly out? Were you butterfly or moth,
my little wild silk?
Something fluttered
on the sonogram,
brought me to the cardiologist, for testing.

Looking out the waiting room window
in the middle of December,
I trained the light of my faith
on the bud of a solitary rose,
its blood-red petals
hanging from a stalk of thorns.
The sight of it got me through
the four weeks I'd have to wait for news
of veins, ventricles, chambers and beats.

We didn't know then how you, at only three,
would get your grandmother through her tests,
how the warmth and light of you would
strengthen her heart.
We didn't know what the tests would show.

We only knew that God had sent us a rose
and we were blessed.

N anabelle was known for her wisdom, and her favorite
song was "Young at Heart." She'd raised a faith-filled
family, was known for her time-tested love for God and
formidable perseverance. She was a trailblazer in her
community, workplace, and church, and had been honored for
her varied accomplishments. But when eldest son, at three
years old, asked her, "Nana, who are you?" she answered
without hesitation, "I'm a mother." Without missing a beat, she
crystalized her identity in a way so akin to the example of Our
Heavenly Mother. She had a foretaste of this meant-to-be
identity when she was just a little girl, in the defining moment
of my grandmother's life. She referred to it as the day she first
felt God loving her. In my grandmother's own words, which I
faithfully recorded:

> "When I was about six or seven, we had a wonderful
> Christmas; I had been given what I most wanted: a
> baby doll and a doll carriage. But we had a very bad
> winter so I could never take the doll carriage out
> because the weather was bad. Finally, one beautiful
> day in the spring, my mother said, 'You can take the
> carriage out.' I remember this so well: I can recall
> her taking the carriage down the steps and
> straightening the carriage's satin cover with the clip
> on it. I remember starting to walk down the street. I
> was always cold when I was little, and this day, I felt
> the sun warming me. I heard the cheerful bell of the
> junkman's horse and carriage coming down the
> street. I walked along with my doll carriage with
> such pure joy that I have never felt again in my life.
> Many years later I read a book written by a priest
> about seeing God in all things. He told the story of a
> woman gardening, with the dirt in her hands and
> the sun warming her; and how she suddenly became
> aware of a different, overwhelming feeling that had
> never come over her before: of security, of beauty. I

remembered that unique feeling from when I was a girl, that day with my doll carriage. I told my brother, a priest, and he said, 'You know what that feeling was? That was God loving you.'"

Uncle T., her brother, went on to say that such a feeling takes you by surprise; it is something you can recognize but not orchestrate. C.S. Lewis called this feeling being "surprised by joy."

Sometimes it takes childlike innocence to fully accept God's love. But like my grandmother, if we can truly, completely accept the love God has for us, we will also become younger at heart, less bogged down by bitterness or anxiety.

It is no wonder that at her 100th birthday party, we played Frank Sinatra's, "Young at Heart," her favorite. It's such a fitting song for her as it reflects the way she lived. In many ways, she was not only the wisest but the youngest heart I've ever known: quick to laugh, fun to be with, and always full of life and agapic love. And all, I assert, because from a very early age she fully and unreservedly accepted the gift of God's love for her. She kept that childlike heart of hope all her days.

My grandmother recalled feeling God's presence loving her for the first time when she was just a little girl, pushing a treasured doll carriage in the warm sunlight. And she would be the first to say that as she grew, she came to feel God loving her in all the people He sent her way. What a beautiful arc this made: from the light of the sun to the light of loved faces. Nanabelle's first memory of God's light as she pushed the carriage was also foreshadowing: her life has always been one of valuing new life and the children she was blessed to influence.

The Child's Blessing

Two children she influenced were my own, who though only five and three when she passed away still talk about her and share stories of her: she made a big impression. To keep her memory fresh, we keep her picture at our breakfast table and remind each other of times we spent with her. While we always say how blessed we were that she was an active part of their lives as a centenarian, it is also true that each of my sons gave her a blessing.

In the case of my youngest son, his picture was displayed in her room at rehab after she broke her hip. We visited her often there, and my sons witnessed her faith, courage and humor in-between therapy sessions at 100 years old. She was so brave, and we were proud of her. One day she pointed at the picture of him on her table. His apple cheeks were spread in a peaceful, steady smile and his round eyes looked directly at the viewer with a peaceful light. Below his little chin and neck was a blue flowered bow tie on a blue collared shirt and he wore khaki pants, his feet bare. "He gets me through," she said. "I focus on that face and I'm encouraged to keep going. He's a blessing, that boy." She didn't say this once or twice. She said it often and with great gratitude. When he visited she'd laugh and smile. When I was still pregnant with him, the doctors thought he might have a heart defect. I had to go for one sonogram after the next to make sure he wouldn't need emergency surgery at birth, or worse, die in-utero. It was a scary time. It was such a beautiful irony that this child whose heart we'd worried so much about was now lifting the heart of his centenarian grandmother as she went through rehabilitation for a broken hip.

After she recovered, God granted her precious healthy months in which we were able to visit her and the children were able to make memories with her. Over a year later when she fell again we brought the boys to see her in the hospital. It was just three days before she died. This time it was my oldest son who gave the blessing. He loved her, wanted to protect her, had visited her often, and also looked up to her. Yet, despite the fact that she was nearly 102 years old, and he was only five years old, he prayed this at her side "Dear God, please bless this little girl." She listened, her eyes fixed intently on him, and she smiled.

At that moment, my son had noticed the eternal youth and beauty in the sage. He effortlessly understood the agelessness of one truly young at heart. I'm reminded of the words of Cary Grant's character, an angel named Dudley, in the film, The Bishop's Wife, to Loretta Young's character, a lovely woman named Julia (a name meaning "youthful," by the way). He tells her: "You never will be old, no matter how old you get. The only people who grow old were born old to begin with."

Then, each of the boys made the sign of the cross on her forehead, as they had been taught, and draped themselves on her in an embrace.

My grandmother would die young at just two months shy of her 102nd birthday. She was the child-like heart who blessed us, and she gathered the blessings of the two youngest ones in the whole family who will forever be blessed in the giving.

Ponder and Pray

- When her young great-grandson invoked a blessing on Nanabelle, what did you think? When he asked Nanabelle, "Who are you," his question was so deep and surprising; her answer so pure. How was their conversation one that transcended the ordinary and became soul to soul?

- Nanabelle's youngest great-grandson's picture inspired her during her rehabilitation. Have you ever been inspired to keep going by looking at a print, painting or photograph? What person in your life makes you want to keep on persevering?

Let us pray with the pure trust of a child: The Prayer of Trust in the Sacred Heart of Jesus by St. Margaret Mary Alacoque:

Jesus, I believe in Your personal love for one so sinful and worthless as I am.

(Repeat after each of the following: Heart of Jesus, I put my trust in You.)

I believe that Your love for me is from all eternity and that it is as tender as a mother's love.

I believe that You have lovingly and wisely planned everything that shall ever happen to me.

I will never seek pleasure forbidden by You and will never lose heart in my efforts to be good.

I will accept the crosses of life as I accept its joys, with a grateful heart, and I will always pray, "Your holy will be done in all things."

I will not be worried or anxious about anything, for I know You will take care of me.

However weak or sinful I may be, I will never doubt Your mercy.

In all my temptations...
In all my weakness...
In all my sorrows...
In every discouragement...
In all my undertakings...
In life and in death...

Heart of love, I put all my trust in you; for I fear all things from my own weakness, but I hope for all things from Your goodness.

Heart of Jesus, our peace and reconciliation, have mercy on us.

"Assumption of Mary"
Juan de Jesus Munera Ochoa

The Lesson of The Last Labor

"My soul rests in God alone from who comes my salvation." –Psalm 62:2

"Star of Bethlehem"
Bruno Piglhein

Faith

for JMFS

Three months before your time, my child, you moved
head down into position, ripe for birth.
The world outside was unseen and unproved—
but still you leaped as though you sensed its worth
and wanted it. And though your world was dark,
removed from any touch except my hand
passing above your solitary ark—
you ate from my own blood; your cosmos spanned
my womb. Responding to my voice, you danced.
So someday when you're grown and faced with doubt
because of grief or age, by fear enhanced—
remember how you once moved towards an out
you could not see. Wait—new life will begin.
Feel God's warm hand above earth's starry skin.

My grandmother taught me many lessons during her life, and one last precious one as she passed away. But let me begin with a story. Before my first son was born, two doctors had remarked that once he found the right position for birth, head down, he waited there for three months, staying in position as though he knew there was something on the outside, and he would find it. This is so much like our experience of faith, and of belief in Heaven. "Blessed are they who have not seen and yet believed," Jesus tells us. A child in utero cannot see the face of its mother, and only hears echoes of her voice. A child's world in utero is so very different from the world he will encounter after birth. How could he ever imagine what awaits? Yet, he senses there is something worthwhile waiting for him... and gets into position with great, pure faith that something beyond exists.

When a woman is pregnant, in her third trimester, she can gently press on her stomach and her unborn child will return the press. This touch is nothing like the close embrace that awaits once the child is born, but it's a beautiful foretaste. There are ways that God touches us now, and just like an unborn child believes there is something beyond that they want to get to... we trust there is something beyond this world, too. Surely, this is what one does who dies in faith.

On December 26, 2018, immediately following the celebration of the birth of the Christ Child, my grandmother, "Nanabelle" was born to eternal life. In her final hours, she received Last Rites and blessings from our parish priest and deacon, and her hospital room was filled with all six of her children and even some of her grandchildren. Each took turns reading Scripture and leading prayers and hymns. When it was my turn, I read from Luke 23:39-43, and as I read these words: *"'Jesus, remember me when You come into Your kingdom!' And He said to him, 'Truly, I say to you, today you will be with Me in*

Paradise,'" I hoped to give her the comfort and assurance she had thought to give her dying friend, Mrs. L, in *her* final hours.

As she passed, I was blessed to be holding her right hand as my mother held her left hand. Others were close by her side and at her feet. So many members of our House of the Sacred Heart were gathered near her and prayed together. As I watched her, I thought of the phrase, "born to eternal life." The final lesson my grandmother taught me is this: The process of dying is a kind of labor, akin to birthing a new life.

Something about the way she breathed that last hour, although waning, was impressive in its focus. The thing I can best liken it to is being in labor. I can attest that when you are in labor, there are moments you'd swear you were dying, such is the pain the body feels as it assists in giving new life. A mother must focus her breathing and ride the labor. This was the woman who loved to remind that "no one is closer to God than a woman in labor." As I held her hand, and knelt at the side of this woman who had herself given birth six times, as I prayed silently again and again, on her behalf, "Jesus, remember me when You come into Your Kingdom," I recognized that she was again very close to God, as her breathing and extreme focus was like that of one in labor while God prepared to birth her into eternal life.

My eldest son once asked, "Nanabelle, who are you?" She immediately replied: "I'm a mother." And, of course, a mother assists God in the growing of new life. Nanabelle was a mother unto the end. As I watched her die, I was privileged not only to witness her faith, but to learn that death is a kind of labor, the kind a mother understands will assist in the bringing of God's new life. My grandmother realized that she had to enter the labor of death in order to reach that new life. Surely, she felt God's warm hand above earth's starry skin.

Ponder and Pray

- Have you learned an important lesson from a loved one who was dying or at their deathbed? Or have you heard a story of someone's noble death that impacted you?

- Have you ever thought of death as a birth? When you hear the phrase "born to eternal life" what comes to mind?

- Jesus tells us in Scripture that the Kingdom of Heaven belongs to such as the little children. Knowing this, how does the prayer from Psalm 131, "Humble Trust in God" and the poem relate to our final perseverance?

- What line in the poem moves you most and why?

Let us pray:

Humble Trust in God

LORD, my heart is not proud;
nor are my eyes haughty.
I do not busy myself with great matters,
with things too sublime for me.
Rather, I have stilled my soul,
Like a weaned child to its mother,
weaned is my soul.
Israel, hope in the LORD,
now and forever.

Heart of Jesus, Victim for sin, have mercy on us.

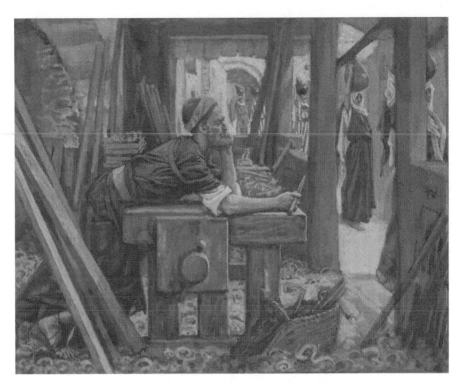

"The Anxiety of Saint Joseph"
James Tissot

The Lesson of The Renovation

"Everyone who listens to these words of mine and acts on them will be like a wise man who built his house on rock. The rain fell, the floods came, and the winds blew and buffeted the house. But it did not collapse: it had been set solidly on rock."
–Mt 7:24-25

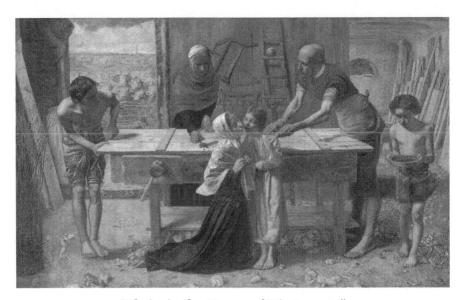

"Christ in the House of His Parents"
John Everett Millais

A Time to Rend and Sew

I. A Time to Rend

(Job Addresses God)

> "Then Job began to tear his cloak and cut off his
> hair" (Job 1:20)

The silence is all. Though I want to split
the stillness of this day with fractured cries,
and tear this room apart, I will admit
that such a sundering would not be wise.
What would it do to shatter every dish,
or smash the vases, break each cup and bowl?
How would that change what I've begun to wish—
that I could go right back to being whole—
even if it meant forgetting you and
the great pain that loving you has brought?—
I tore my hair today. You understand?
My clothing, too. I wait for you to cry
out, ask me not to harm myself. I won't.
But I know loneliness. And God, you don't.

II. A Time to Sew

(God Answers Job)

> "Who is this that obscures divine plans with words
> of ignorance? Where were you when I founded the
> earth?" (Job 38:2,4)

You say I don't know loneliness. What, Job,
you've never seen the chasms between stars?
Observe the distance of your heart, then probe
yourself for answers. Look down at your scars.
You think I put them there, I know. But pain
is from your world, not mine. And all the while
I plan my entrance. Gardens all need rain
to raise their beauty. My plot grows a trial
of such deep suffering, the torn curtain
of a great temple will be how I rend
the earth of sleep. Sacrifice makes certain
a love that will not hesitate or end.
Mend yourself, now. Follow my command.
(I'm pierced in ways you'll never understand.)

The Renovation

Because of the love and the lessons learned within it, my grandmother's Red House became a legend to which I always wanted to find my way back. When my grandmother moved out of her house to move in with my Aunt B. and her family, I began to have a recurring dream about returning to the Red House. I would dream of breaking in through a window and finding it just as it had been when she'd lived there. I'd be back at that kitchen table again, while she poured the tea. Other times, I'd dream the house was empty and I was filling it once more with the furniture she had given away. This was a dream I shared with my children, frequently telling them of my urge to return to that place which had meant so much and wishing I could bring them into those hallowed rooms.

When my grandmother moved out, she gave her things away to her children, dividing furniture and paintings and linens among them, basing her choices on which objects were dearest to each of them. Among the many items they were each given, Aunt G. inherited the corner cabinet where Nanabelle had kept the jars of candy she shared with the grandchildren; Uncle B. received the Regulator clock; Uncle E. got the kitchen table and round-backed chairs; my mother got the rocker that Grandpapa had always sat in to shine his shoes; Uncle G. was given the gold-framed still life of the red flowers, and Aunt B. received the wooden statue of St. Joseph, which she placed on her piano. As these and other objects from our House of the Sacred Heart were integrated into each new home, they blessed and became part of the stories there, helping each of the next generation's homes to become a new House of the Sacred Heart, especially as each continued the lessons they had learned in the Red House of faith, hope, and charity.

Over fifteen years after my grandmother moved out of the Red House, and just one year after her death, my uncle purchased it; then, with the help of his siblings repaired it. My uncle set about restoring the charm and beauty of the family's heart. It was a gift he gave the entire family, bringing back something we thought was gone forever. He returned the pulse to our House of the Sacred Heart as he hung Nanabelle's Regulator clock back up in the home, and moved his table into the kitchen bay window. He set out pictures of all generations of the family, and opened the Bible in his living room, as though he was welcoming each family member back in once more, and praying for us all. Then, my uncle hung pictures of the Sacred Heart of Jesus and the Immaculate Heart of Mary.

After much mourning of Nanabelle's death, I could not believe that I was now being given the grace of returning to the Red House, of entering under that roof again, this time with my husband and our children. I brought my family to visit the sacred place that had for so long been just a memory. My sons told Uncle B, "Thank you for making my mother's dream come true." I leaned against its walls, and recalled the words of St. Therese: "If I cannot see the brilliance of your Face or hear your sweet voice, O my God, I can live by your grace, I can rest in your Sacred Heart!"

Ecclesiastes teaches that there is a time to rend, and a time to sew. Our family had certainly known the time to rend: the grief, the loss of people we loved and even the loss of the Red House. But we also experienced the time to sew: holding on to memories, moving forward in joy and hope, and now this greatest kind of time to sew: my Uncle B literally fixing my grandmother's home up again, mending and repairing where needed, and returning the charm and beauty of the place. It was as though he had stitched a wound closed.

Ponder and Pray

- What repairs are needed in your life?

- How might you begin reparation for the destruction of right relationships; or for order in your life or your faith? Think and pray on this.

- Was anyone or any event responsible for a drastic change in your life that moved you forward in faith and healing unexpectedly?

- Was there ever something very dear to you that someone else fixed? Explain.

- How are we called to make reparation to the Sacred Heart?

- When was the last time you received the Sacrament of Reconciliation/Confession to make the needed renovations to your soul?

Let us pray the Traditional Prayer of Reparation to the Sacred Heart

My loving Jesus, out of the grateful love I bear you, and to make reparation for my unfaithfulness to grace, I give You my heart, and I consecrate myself wholly to You; and with Your help I purpose to sin no more.

Amen.

Let us pray The Holy Hour of Reparation

"THE SACRED HEART OF JESUS... began this devotion of the Holy Hour of Reparation, when He entered the Garden of Gethsemane on Mount Olivet. He said to His Apostles: 'My soul is sorrowful even unto death. Stay ye here and watch with Me.' Later He said to them: 'Could ye not watch one hour with Me? Watch and pray, that ye enter not into temptation.'" [Matt. 26:38, 40, 41]

As Jesus spoke to His Apostles, so He pleads with us to stay and watch and pray with Him. His Sacred Heart is filled with sadness, because so many doubt Him, despise Him, insult Him, ridicule Him, spit upon Him, slap Him, accuse Him, condemn Him. In the Sacrament of His Love, so many forget Him. Every mortal sin brings down the terrible scourges on His Sacred Body, presses the sharp thorns into His Sacred Head, and hammers the cruel nails into His Sacred Hands and Feet. The ingratitude of mankind continually pierces His Sacred Heart.

When Jesus saw the sins of the world and the reparation that must be made to His Heavenly Father, He began to fear and to be sad and sorrowful. "Kneeling down, He prayed: 'Father, if Thou will, remove this chalice from Me; But not My Will, Thine be done: There appeared an Angel from Heaven to strengthen Him; and being in agony, He prayed the longer, and His sweat became as drops of blood trickling to the ground." [Lk 22:41, 44]

The Sacred Heart of Jesus said to St. Margaret Mary: "Make reparation for the ingratitude of men. Spend an hour in prayer to appease Divine justice, to implore mercy for sinners, to honor Me, to console Me for My bitter suffering when abandoned by My Apostles, when they did not WATCH ONE HOUR WITH ME."

-From the "Soul Assurance Prayer Plan," copyright 1945. I encourage you to read and pray the full Holy Hour of prayers, published in 1945, available through CMJ Marian Publishers. If your church will begin offering these prayers of reparation through a Holy Hour on Wednesday evenings, even better!

Heart of Jesus, salvation of those who trust in Thee, have mercy on us.

"Sacred Heart of Jesus"
Pompeo Batoni

The Lesson of The Song

"A thousand years in your eyes are merely a day gone by. Before a watch passes in the night you wash them away." —Psalm 90:4-5

"The Laundry Woman"
Camille Pissarro

Work Song

They say that those who sing, pray twice. What, then,
of those who sing a prayer and also work?
I'd say that they pray thrice. At only ten,
my grandmother came home from school to lurk,
hiding behind a wall, to listen in
to hear her mother washing clothes by hand,
and as she'd scrub against the board, she'd sing
a song about how Jesus understands
how hard we labor, how He gives the night,
enfolding us with curtains made of stars,
the way He lets us rest to set it right–
the way He mends, makes beauty from our scars.
Years later, worn by age, she still could hear
her mother singing, sense God's presence near.

How far must we go back through the generations to give thanks to those who, because they loved and labored, our lives were able to have meaning? Nanabelle's mother, whom the little ones called "Nanny," was a strong, faith-filled matriarch with ten children and over forty grandchildren and so there were many stories about her told to me as I grew. She and her husband, known as "Poppy," even took in a niece when her parents died in the Spanish Flu pandemic, in spite of their full nest. Poppy was a police detective, and had served as a motorcycle officer, a mounted officer, and also "walked a beat," though he said his prayers each night on his knees. He demonstrated valor, sacrifice, and faith. He brought my Grandpapa on retreats with him each year on the day after Thanksgiving, a tradition my Grandpapa continued into his old age. Nanny and Poppy were so proud that all their children were faith-filled and that their eldest son had become a wonderful priest. Nanny once told Nanabelle, "When my time comes I'll be ready. I've done my work. All my children know God, love God, and serve God."

Nanny was the daughter of "Grandma Kelly", who had been born in Ireland. At Grandma Kelly's funeral, dozens of people lined the street wearing mourning bands and watching the horse-drawn hearse pass. Family legend recounts they all owed her money. Though Grandma Kelly was a humble washer-woman, who took in the washing and ironing of the wealthy, though she scrimped and saved and lived in a tiny apartment with her husband, she gave out money to anyone who was in need. This strong Irish-immigrant heritage of humility and hard work had forged Nanny's character, but she learned to cook from a German woman, which made for meals that were tasty and hearty. This was an age before television, clothes washers and dryers. The work each day that piled up for Nanny must have been overwhelming. Meals were made from scratch. Entertainment centered around the whole family: card games like euchre, and nightly gatherings around the radio to listen to shows offering music, comedy, and drama. The piano was at the center of the living room and everyone played a musical instrument and sang. In their home was a large, prominent print of "Jesus in Gethsemane" by Heinrich Hofmann, a constant reminder of God. Household chores were many. Laundry was endless, even with meager wardrobes. But opportunities for character-building were also endless... in their capable hands.

During the height of the Great Depression, very often during Nanny's daily chores, men would come to the kitchen door to beg a piece of bread. Nanabelle recalls her mom giving them more than they asked for, spooning out a bowl of soup to these strangers, along with the bread. There was a vivid memory about her mother that Nanabelle loved to share. The story goes that often when my Nanabelle was home from school, but before her mother knew she'd arrived, she'd see Nanny doing the laundry, using the washboard and wash bucket, and as she would rhythmically press the sudsy clothes against the metal-ribbed board, bending over her labors, she would sing a song of love calling upon the Sacred Heart of Jesus. Nanabelle would hide for just a moment, so as not to interrupt the beautiful song, sung in her mother's lovely voice. This same mother had buried a child of four years old, with blond curls and blue eyes, who had died of pneumonia. She had gone three years not knowing if her priest son had been killed in the Philippines. She had broken down with sorrow at her father's funeral, knowing he had died alone, quarantined with tuberculosis, and she his beloved daughter had only been allowed to wave at him, where he sat in a wheelchair on a hospital porch. She didn't mope about or stay in bed all day, though she had many a reason to. She got out of bed, put one foot in front of the next, and got busy doing what was needed, a ministry of domestic giving, a great lifelong pouring-out of self.

The lyrics Nanny sang include these: "Night folds its starry curtains round...Loving God, how sweet thou art, to call us from your cares a while, to rest within your Sacred Heart." One of the sweetest things Nanabelle ever told me was one Sunday after I had cantored at Mass. She said, "Your singing reminds me of my mother. You have the same tone to your voice that she had."

Nanny sang while she washed the laundry. Her cheerfulness while working left such an impression on her daughter, Nanabelle: that the mother of ten children could find joy in the midst of a simple task that many would consider drudgery. Nanabelle also told us how Nanny's song transcended the work, through the simple love she brought to it.

St. Therese of Lisieux wrote that she often felt the greatest insights and responses to her prayers came during her daily work. Little did Nanny know that she would provide inspiration to those who heard of her joyful and humble approach to work. Nanny was just living her faith, drawing from it the strength she needed as a reminder that all cares and worries she may have been burdened with, would all pass on or be put into their proper perspective when resting for a spell within the Sacred Heart.

Ponder and Pray

- Nanny's lovely habit of singing a hymn of praise to the Sacred Heart while washing the clothes made a lasting impression on her oldest daughter, Nanabelle. What was it in Nanabelle's character that recognized this as a holy ritual and held its meaning in her heart? Do you have a similar memory?

- Do you ever find yourself singing a hymn or song of faith during a menial task?

Let us pray, in the words of the Evening Hymn to the Sacred Heart

Night folds her starry curtains round, As day hath faded on the hills, And thro' the silence so profound, calm peace a fragrant balm distills.

A soothing voice like incense falls, All cares, all sorrows to beguile; Our Lord in love and pity calls, 'Come to my heart and rest a while.' Not man, nor angel can portray, O dearest Lord, how sweet Thou art, to call us from our cares away, to rest within Thy Sacred Heart!

To serve Thee, Jesus, is to reign; Thy blessed bondage makes us free; We count it as our highest gain, Forsaking all to follow Thee.

Thrice happy are the hours and bright we spend beneath Thy dear control; Thy yoke is sweet, Thy burden light; Thy love the sunshine of the soul.

Not man, nor angel can portray, O dearest Lord, how sweet Thou art, To call us from our cares away, To rest within Thy Sacred Heart!

Heart of Jesus, hope of those who die in Thee, have mercy on us.

"The Middleburg Altar" (detail)
Rogier van der Weyden

The Lesson of The New House of the Sacred Heart

"A great and wondrous sign appeared in heaven: a woman clothed with the sun, with the moon under her feet and a crown of twelve stars on her head. She was pregnant..." –Rev 12:1

"Star of Bethlehem"
Elihu Vedder

The House of Stars

When I was just a girl, I dreamed
of flying through a blue-black sky—
the stars were clearer, closer
than I've ever seen them before.
I've never seen a shooting star,
I said aloud, *but always wanted to.*
Just then one fell before me, in a rush—
then another—
each a stark snowflake,
a mirror-ball.
Then the sky turned still,
and very slowly,
the constellation of a house—
a pointed roof, windows and a door—
glided before me.
I founded my home upon the star
of the wise men, and hoped to shine
a light for all who'd come across our door—
a beam upon the Babe of Bethlehem.

Night folds its starry curtains round." Thus begins the hymn my great-grandmother sang while she washed her family's humble curtains, sheets, and clothes. That hymn sung back beginning in 1925 and nearly forgotten today made it through the generations to my ears and my children's. It has taught that six generations later, love for God and a special devotion to the Sacred Heart at the root of our family tree has been passed down, like a healing sap to nourish us no matter what drought we endure.

In 2020 when the pandemic came, and Masses said in-person were disallowed, the natural hunger and thirst we have for the Eucharist and the Sacrifice of the Mass crescendoed like a waiting song of longed-for love. Each soul had to stand before God in prayer and ask if he or she had appreciated the Real Presence of the Eucharist as much as possible before it was denied. Different family members described the experience we had all shared in their own ways: "I feel lost without Communion;" "I never thought something like this would happen, like I'm being denied my very home;" "if this ever ends, I'll go to daily Masses whenever I can and not just Mass on Sunday;" "When I next receive my Lord I will kneel down to show my surrendered pride, my full-hearted humility and gratitude, my desperation for the King." Our hunger for the Eucharist was one and the same with our hunger for the Sacred Heart. St. Margaret Mary reminds that the Sacred Heart is the Holy Eucharist. When we view an image of Jesus extending his Sacred Heart, we might as well see him offering us the Host.

That is why it was particularly meaningful that the first Sunday that churches near us re-opened was the Feast of Corpus Christi. We attended Confession, Mass, and Eucharistic Adoration and a Corpus Christi Procession. Filing outside the chapel and following the Eucharist in the golden monstrance, held high, with the fringed canopy above it, singing hymns and praying together, through a warm summer field under a vibrant blue sky was the most beautiful way to celebrate our first reception of the Eucharist in months that I could have imagined. Walking through that field, marching behind the Real Presence of Our Lord, all of us stopping from time to time, to kneel down and pray, then rising and joining once more in song... I felt the thrill of what it must have been to follow Jesus during the years of his earthly ministry, across all kinds of terrain: sharing fellowship, singing, praying and adoring his company, all the while.

After the lockdowns had lifted, and the surreal spring gave way to summer, we decided to bless our home and land and offer all we had, in prayer, to the Father. It was one year, almost exactly, since we'd hosted our parish priest for dinner and had an Enthronement Ceremony, in which we "solemnly enthroned the Sacred Heart of Jesus," making the Sacred Heart of Jesus the King of our family and home and displaying newly-blessed images of the Sacred Heart of Jesus and Immaculate Heart of Mary in a prominent place within our home.

Part of the Prayer of Thanksgiving that we all prayed together to close the ceremony included these words, "O most faithful Friend, had You been here in the midst of sorrow, our tears would have been less bitter; the comforting balm of peace would then have soothed these hidden wounds, which are known to You alone. Come, for even now, perhaps, there is drawing near for us the twilight of tribulation, and the decline of the passing days of our youth and our illusions. Stay with us, for it is already late, and a sinful world seeks to envelop us in the darkness of its denials while we wish to adhere to You who alone are the Way, the Truth, and the Life. Repeat for us those words You uttered of old: This day I must abide in this home." Little did we know when we prayed those words of the coming pandemic, the "social distancing" from loved ones, rampant political unrest, and worst of all, the barring of church doors, the stopping of the Sacraments, deemed by governors and mayors and even some church leaders as "non-essential." Yet we had asked the Sacred Heart to take up His abode with us, to live within our home even as we live within His.

So, lo and behold, one weary year later, as my husband and I blessed our home and land, offering it to the Father, we felt freer when it was done, happier, renouncing any claim to our property beyond what pleases the Eternal Father and offering our home to serve in whatever way God wishes. The very next day after we did this, I was contacted with a wonderful opportunity. I was asked if I would be willing to give shelter to a Missionary Image of Our Lady of Guadalupe for three days and two nights. We immediately said yes. It was all the more poignant to us because two and a half years earlier, we had moved into our home and had it blessed by a great priest on December 8, the Feast of Our Lady of Guadalupe. That day, we named our home "Star Manor," after the star the wise men followed to Jesus. It would be a daily reminder to our children that "Wise Men Still Seek Him," and that we should live our lives in a manner that, like the Magi, follows the Bethlehem Star. Star Manor by its name also evokes the stars on Mary's Guadalupe veil. To have Our Lady's Missionary image visit Star Manor, a house that had first been blessed on the Feast of Our Lady of Guadalupe, was a gift of joy beyond measure. "Joy to the World," that famous Christmas carol, resounds "Let every heart prepare Him room." We now prepared room for our Lady of Guadalupe, a sacred image of Mary pregnant with our Lord. There would be room for her in our inn, and we trusted she would lead us, ever more deeply, to the Sacred Heart of her Son.

Ponder and Pray

- Does your home have a name? If it doesn't, what might you name it?

- Is your house dedicated/consecrated to God? Is your home a safe haven? Is it a refuge of the Sacred Heart? Is it the home in Bethany where Jesus can rest awhile? What do you need to do to improve its meaning for yourself and others?

- Does your home display images of the Sacred Heart of Jesus and the Immaculate Heart of Mary? What moves you when you look upon an image of the Sacred and Immaculate Hearts?

- What is a key element that your home has already to draw Christ in?

- What does the Eucharist mean to you? Do you have a story of finding solace in the Eucharist?

Let us pray the Act of Consecration to the Sacred Heart of Jesus

I give myself and consecrate to the Sacred Heart of our Lord Jesus Christ, my person and my life, my actions, pains and sufferings, so that I may be unwilling to make use of any part of my being other than to honor, love and glorify the Sacred Heart. This is my unchanging purpose, namely, to be all His, and to do all things for the love of Him, at the same time renouncing with all my heart whatever is displeasing to Him. I therefore take You, O Sacred Heart, to be the only object of my love, the guardian of my life, my assurance of salvation, the remedy of my weakness and inconstancy, the atonement for all the faults of my life and my sure refuge at the hour of death.

Be then, O Heart of goodness, my justification before God the Father, and turn away from me the strokes of his righteous anger. O Heart of love, I put all my confidence in You, for I fear everything from my own wickedness and frailty, but I hope for all things from Your goodness and bounty.

Remove from me all that can displease You or resist Your holy will; let your pure love imprint Your image so deeply upon my heart, that I shall never be able to forget You or to be separated from You.

May I obtain from all Your loving kindness the grace of having my name written in Your Heart, for in You I desire to place all my happiness and glory, living and dying in bondage to You. Amen.

Let us pray the Act of the Consecration to the Immaculate Heart of Mary

Most Holy Virgin Mary, tender Mother of men, to fulfill the desires of the Sacred Heart of Jesus and the request of the Vicar of Your Son on earth, we consecrate ourselves and our families to your Sorrowful and Immaculate Heart, O Queen of the Most Holy Rosary, and we recommend to You, all the people of our country and all the world.

Please accept our consecration, dearest Mother, and use us as You wish to accomplish Your designs in the world.

O Sorrowful and Immaculate Heart of Mary, Queen of the Most Holy Rosary, and Queen of the World, rule over us, together with the Sacred Heart of Jesus Christ, Our King. Save us from the spreading flood of modern paganism; kindle in our hearts and homes the love of purity, the practice of a virtuous life, an ardent zeal for souls, and a desire to pray the Rosary more faithfully.

We come with confidence to You, O Throne of Grace and Mother of Fair Love. Inflame us with the same Divine Fire which has inflamed Your own Sorrowful and Immaculate Heart. Make our hearts and homes Your shrine, and through us, make the Heart of Jesus, together with your rule, triumph in every heart and home.

Amen.

Heart of Jesus, delight of all the Saints, have mercy on us.

"Jesus Traveling"
James Tissot

"Sacred Heart of Jesus"
Pompeo Batoni

"Immaculate Heart of Mary"
Leopold Kupelwieser

The Holy Face from the Shroud of Turin

"If my people, which are called by my name, shall humble themselves, and pray, and seek my face, and turn from their wicked ways; then I will hear from heaven, and will forgive their sin, and will heal their land." 2 Chron 7:14

Enthronement of Your Home to the Sacred Heart of Jesus

Sacred Heart of Jesus Enthronement Ceremony:

1. Go to Mass on the day of the Enthronement if possible. Recommendation: have Mass celebrated for the intentions of the family on the day of the Enthronement, or at least attend Mass as a Family and receive Holy Communion on the Sunday prior to the enthronement.

2. Invite a priest. His presence will make this consecration a more solemn occasion, and the ceremony involves prayers and a blessing to be said by him. If a priest is not available, the father or head of the home can lead.

3. Clean and organize your house for the Enthronement. Prepare the altar where the image of the Sacred Heart will be enthroned. Include, if possible, a white cloth, candles, even flowers. Have holy water ready. The Sacred Heart picture or statue should be placed on a small table near this "throne" prior to the ceremony. Dress nicely for the occasion (think "Sunday Best").

4. Invite relatives and friends. All together, gather in the room where the ceremony will take place once the priest arrives.

5. Bless the image of the Sacred Heart of Jesus. It is important to have a priest preside at the ceremony, but when if impossible to have him present, the image can be blessed beforehand.

6. Enthrone the image of the Sacred Heart of Jesus in the place of honor.

7. Pray the Apostles' Creed (out loud and standing) after the blessing, to express the faith of the family.

8. Everyone is seated while the priest or presider addresses a few words to those present.

9. Formula of consecration. This is a form approved by St. Pius X on May 19, 1908 and is required as such to gain the indulgences:

O Sacred Heart of Jesus, Who didst make known to St. Margaret Mary Thine ardent desire to reign over Christian families, behold us assembled here today to proclaim Thine absolute dominion over our home.

Henceforth we purpose to lead a life like unto Thine so that amongst us may flourish the virtues for which Thou didst promise peace on earth, and for this end we will banish from our midst the spirit of the world which Thou dost abhor so much.

Thou wilt reign over our understanding by the simplicity of our faith. Thou wilt reign over our hearts by an ardent love for Thee; and may the flame of this love be ever kept burning in our hearts by the frequent reception of the Holy Eucharist.

Deign, O Divine Heart, to preside over our meetings, to bless our undertakings both spiritual and temporal, to banish all worry and care, to sanctify our joys and soothe our sorrows. If any of us should ever have the misfortune to grieve Thy Sacred Heart, remind him of Thy goodness and mercy towards the repentant sinner.

Lastly when the hour of separation will sound and death will plunge our home into mourning, then shall we all and every one of us be resigned to Thy eternal decrees, and seek consolation in the thought that we shall one day be reunited in Heaven, where we shall sing the praises and blessings of Thy Sacred Heart for all eternity.

May the Immaculate Heart of Mary and the glorious Patriarch St. Joseph offer Thee this our Consecration and remind us of the same all the days of our life. Glory to the Divine Heart of Jesus, our King and our Father!

10. Pray for the deceased members of your family. Pray one Our Father and one Hail Mary for these, and for those who are absent.

11. Consecration of children. Children may recite a poem, sing a hymn, or pray in honor of the Sacred Heart:

Most sweet Jesus, Divine Friend of children, receive our hearts, make them pure, holy and happy; receive also our bodies, our souls, and all our strength. We consecrate ourselves to Thee now and forever. Be Thou alone our King. All our thoughts, and our words, our actions, and our prayers, we consecrate to Thee, our Friend and our King.

12. Final benediction. The priest blesses those present and a certificate of enthronement can be signed by the priest and the family.

"Virgin of Guadalupe"

Afterword: The Starry Mantle

I invited my family to come over for tacos in homage to Guadalupe and to see the Missionary Image.

How I fussed with the house, feeling like Martha in the best of ways, wanting to arrange things nicely for Our Lady. The children rushed to the door in joy and excitement to greet her; my husband went out to help the Missionary worker who had delivered her to carry the heavy weight of it to our door. "Who am I that the Mother of my Lord should come to me?" was the prayer that sprang up in me. On its stand the breathtaking image was life-size and an exact replica of the Guadalupe tilma image displayed in Mexico.

"Am I not here who am your mother?" Our Lady of Guadalupe famously comforted Juan Diego... Juan, John... calling to mind the name of the one given as son at the foot of the cross, the same John who leaned his head against Jesus' Sacred Heart. And of course in the Guadalupe apparition and sacred image, Mary is pregnant with Jesus, holding Our Savior safely and lovingly within her most pure and virginal womb.

We set the miraculous image up in the dining room and when my mom came in, her eyes filled with tears. "Oh!" was the reaction each of us felt, seeing her life-size beauty, Our Lady's presence filling the room: There was a sign that came with the image. It read, *"The Rector of the Basilica of Our Lady of Guadalupe blessed this image and prayed for the success of Our Lady's Mission to bring a culture of life, sanctity of the family, solidarity of the Church in America, and a civilization of love. Pope Saint John Paul II said, 'I feel drawn to the Image of Our Lady because her face is full of kindness and simplicity... it calls me." She calls you, too."*

During the pandemic, I had kept a picture of Nanabelle with the boys at my breakfast table and daily pointed out her face at 100 years old to them. "Look at her eyes," I'd say, "and that smile. Do you think she was a happy person?" "Oh yes! She was always happy!" They'd respond. "And do you know what she lived through? She lived through the Spanish Flu pandemic, The Great Depression, when food and money were scarce, and two World Wars. That's because to her and many other people who were young when she was young, hard times made them stronger, not grumpier. And it made them appreciate what they had. They called Nanabelle's generation, 'The Greatest Generation.' And I think YOU just might be part of the next greatest generation," I'd say, "because you are going through hard times already and we're still a joyful, loving family and we can get through it! You're going to be like Nanabelle!" One of the hardest things for them was being away from whom they call "the members," short for family members. So now that we were having family over to pray and venerate the image, the boys were elated. Anyone who was able to attend did so. It was a family reunion, the first time we had seen each other since the pandemic lockdown began many months prior. Their delight as each person arrived to our home was enormous.

The "Tacos and Tilmas" party was so much fun. It was a beautiful evening: an Annunciation-blue sky, warm sunshine cooled by a breeze, and a garden full of flowers. I set up the food in the garden: chicken and beef tacos, guacamole and salsa. Aunt C brought her Southwest Salad. I made chocolate cupcakes. We sang and celebrated Uncle B's birthday. Conversation in our kitchen was fertile with talk of persevering through humor, creativity, and faith. During the fun, one or two at a time, my family members slipped into the dining room to spend some quiet prayer time with Our Lady in the presence of the Missionary Image. We decided to end the night sitting together in the dining room before the Image of Our Lady and pray a Rosary. The walls resounded with all of our voices melding together. As we journeyed the decades of beads, we prayed for the graces we needed, for health, for our country, for protection and peace. At the end of the Rosary, everyone was visibly moved and keenly aware of our depth of gratitude for each other and for our shared faith.

As we said our last prayer, the spirit of the House of the Sacred Heart felt alive and well in us. Just then, the doorbell rang, and I answered it only to discover that the Our Lady of Guadalupe Rosaries I had ordered for each of them as a little gift to remember the night and our prayerful reunion after a long quarantine, had just arrived. "What are the chances those Rosaries would arrive just at this moment!" several said. "This is Mary's timing!" Each person held their Rosary to the Missionary Image to have their beads blessed as a remembrance of this incredible opportunity.

We said elated goodnights to each other at the end of the evening, each person holding their Guadalupe Rosary. As each person crossed the threshold, the cowbells on our door jangled happily as it was moved open and closed. Each person passed the holy water font and House Blessing picture with the image of Jesus pointing to his Sacred Heart given to us by Nanabelle as a way to celebrate the purchase of our new home. Here's what the prayer at our door says:

> God bless our home both day and night
> And keep it in thy shining light.
> God bless our thoughts, our every task
> And keep them pure and ever steadfast.
>
> God grant us love and peace of mind
> And keep our faith in all mankind.
> God give us strength in time of need
> And keep our hope in Thee, indeed.
>
> God bless all that o'er our threshold pass
> And keep our friendship everlast.
> God bless us all, both young and old
> And keep Thy heavenly home our goal.

What had we learned that night praying the Rosary together at Star Manor? That months of starvation for the Holy Eucharist and church attendance and each other's joyful company had been a sore, challenging test and now that churches had recently reopened and we had rejoined, we had been doubly blessed through this shared Visitation and this time together. We were, together, carrying on what was taught by Nanabelle and Grandpapa and Nanny and Grandma Kelly and all the generations of God-lovers going back for generations. "Keep on doing what you have learned and heard and seen in me... whatever is lovely, true, etc..." Scripture teaches us, and we felt those beloved family members' memory and faith alive and well in us. But there was something else. I felt the beauty of it rising up in me as I put away the food, tucked in and kissed the little sleepyheads, and turned out the lights in the silence of night. At Star Manor, the descendants of the House of the Sacred Heart, within whom the chords of the hymn "Night Folds Its Starry Curtains Round" still echoed in our blood, had gathered together under Mary's starry mantle and begged her through our prayers, to help us remain, always, her children, at her side. And we had been held under her mantle all along. For our truest home, no matter what befalls us, is the Heart of Jesus. And Mary, after all, is the first dwelling place of Our Lord's Sacred Heart; she is the "Tabernacle of God." Our Lady, then, is the first House of the Sacred Heart, and she had gathered us under her mantle.

The next morning, saddened that the Missionary Image would leave my home, I turned to prayer to comfort me. My prayer, as I helped to pack up the image entreated the Immaculate Heart of Mother Mary that her presence would remain in my home in a stronger way than before this visit. The next guardian of the image arrived to pick it up and bring it to a church, for a special Mass. He noticed I was wearing a medal of the Holy Face, and gave me, as a gift, a beautiful image of the Holy Face, which I framed and hung over a print of Our Lady of Guadalupe, in the dining room right where the image had stood. Remembering that Mary is pregnant in the Guadalupe image, and that she always leads us to her Son, it was no surprise that the comfort I was brought came in the form of the Holy Face of Jesus. I remembered again how I was cautioned as a little girl by Grandpapa to respect and honor the Dogwood blossom which bore the wounds of Christ and stoked my wonder and awe for the crown of thorns hiding in plain sight in the blooms of a backyard tree. Here I was now so many years later placing an image of the Holy Face of Jesus with His Holy Crown in the center of my home, to honor the wounds he bore for us.

On the mantel of our kitchen there is a song clock and at each hour, a hymn rings out. "Ave Maria," "In the Garden," "Jesus Loves Me," "What a Friend We Have in Jesus," and "How Great Thou Art." Each time that last song resounds through our walls, I think of Nanabelle and Grandpapa, the lessons I learned in Our House of the Sacred Heart and I join my grandfather in prayerfully bowing to Our Lord. In the living room of Star Manor, we have a beautiful statue of the Sacred Heart, his arms open in an embrace, inviting my children on more than one occasion to carefully hug it. The displayed heart is wonderfully detailed, and the face of Jesus is both tender and strong. During the course of our busy day, we pause sometimes to gaze at His Holy Face and his beautiful Sacred Heart. Our very glance of love and longing is our prayer. Dear Lord, may the song and sense and soul of prayer pervade our home for the rest of our days. And may we continue to see the signs and symbols You leave us.

Our devotion to the Sacred Heart, our desire to rest within His Heart forever, impels us to gaze upon his Holy Face, and to seek that our own hearts, like precious coins belonging to the treasury of heaven will bear the image of our Lord's Holy Face. As St. Therese of Lisieux wrote, "Your Image, O my Savior blest, Upon my heart imprint in fire, Divine bouquet which I love best. My only wealth—Your Holy Face, 'Tis Heaven on this earth for me... to you I'll soon draw every heart."

No matter where we live or where we go, may Our Lady enfold us under her starry, Holy Mantle. May we entrust everything to Jesus and seek his face. And may we take refuge in the chambers of His Sacred Heart.

"One thing I ask from the Lord,
this only do I seek:
that I may dwell in the house of the Lord
all the days of my life,
to gaze on the beauty of the Lord
and to seek him in his temple." –Psalm 27

Let us pray to Mary Our Lady of Guadalupe, and ask that she pray for us as we prepare to consecrate ourselves to the Sacred Heart of Our Lord Jesus Christ.

Dear mother, we love you. We thank you for your promise to help us in our need. We trust in your love that dries our tears and comforts us. Teach us to find our peace in your Son, Jesus, and bless us every day of our lives.

Help us to build a shrine in our hearts. Make it as beautiful as the one built for you on the mount of Tepeyac. A shrine full of trust, hope, and love of Jesus growing stronger each day.

Mary, you have chosen to remain with us by giving us your most wonderful and holy self-image on Juan Diego's cloak. May we feel your loving presence as we look upon your face. Like Juan, give us the courage to bring your message of hope to everyone.

You are our mother and our inspiration. Hear our prayers and answer us.

Amen.

an excerpt from the Prayer of Thanksgiving to the Sacred Heart of Jesus

"Glory be to You, O Sacred Heart of Jesus... May our home be for You a haven as sweet as that of Bethany, where You can find rest in the midst of loving friends, who like Mary have chosen the better part in the loving intimacy of Your Heart! May this home be for You, O beloved Saviour, a humble but hospitable refuge during the exile imposed on You by Your enemies. Come then, Lord Jesus, come, for here as at Nazareth, we have a tender love for the Virgin Mary, Your sweet Mother whom You have given us to be our Mother whom You have given us to be our Mother. Come to fill with Your sweet presence the vacancies which misfortune and death have wrought in our midst. O most faithful Friend, had You been here in the midst of sorrow, our tears would have been less bitter; the comforting balm of peace would then have soothed these hidden wounds, which are known to You alone. Come, for even now, perhaps, there is drawing near for us the twilight of tribulation, and the decline of the passing days of our youth and our illusions. Stay with us, for it is already late, and a sinful world seeks to envelop us in the darkness of its denials while we wish to adhere to You who alone are the Way the Truth and the Life. Repeat for us those words You uttered of old: This day I must abide in this home."

Amen.

"Christ's Farewell to Mary" (as He begins His ministry)
Piotr Stachiewicz

The Litany of the Sacred Heart of Jesus

Priest: Lord, have mercy on us.

All: Christ, have mercy on us.

Priest: Lord, have mercy on us. Christ, hear us.

All: Christ, graciously hear us.

Priest: God, the Father of Heaven,

All: Have mercy on us.

God, the Son, Redeemer of the world, have mercy on us.

God, the Holy Ghost,

Holy Trinity, one God,

Heart of Jesus, Son of the Eternal Father,

Heart of Jesus, formed by the Holy Ghost in the Womb of the Virgin Mother,

Heart of Jesus, substantially united to the Word of God,

Heart of Jesus, of Infinite Majesty,

Heart of Jesus, Holy Temple of God,

Heart of Jesus, Tabernacle of the Most High,

Heart of Jesus, House of God and Gate of Heaven,

Heart of Jesus, burning furnace of Charity,

Heart of Jesus, abode of Justice and Love,

Heart of Jesus, full of Goodness and Love,

Heart of Jesus, abyss of all virtues,

Heart of Jesus, most worthy of all praise, have mercy on us.

Heart of Jesus, King and Center of all hearts,

Heart of Jesus, in Whom are all the treasures of wisdom and knowledge,

Heart of Jesus, in Whom dwells the fullness of Divinity,

Heart of Jesus, in Whom the Father was well pleased,

Heart of Jesus, of Whose fullness we have all received,

Heart of Jesus, desire of the everlasting hills,

Heart of Jesus, patient and most merciful,

Heart of Jesus, enriching all who invoke Thee,

Heart of Jesus, fountain of life and holiness,

Heart of Jesus, propitiation for our sins,

Heart of Jesus, loaded down with reproaches,

Heart of Jesus, bruised for our offences,

Heart of Jesus, obedient unto death,

The Litany of the Sacred Heart of Jesus

Heart of Jesus, pierced with a lance,

Heart of Jesus, source of all consolation,

Heart of Jesus, our life and resurrection,

Heart of Jesus, our peace and reconciliation,

Heart of Jesus, Victim for sin,

Heart of Jesus, salvation of those who trust in Thee,

Heart of Jesus, hope of those who die in Thee,

Heart of Jesus, delight of all the Saints,

Priest: Lamb of God, Who takest away the sins of the world,

All: Spare us, O Lord.

Priest: Lamb of God, Who takest away the sins of the world,

All: Graciously hear us, O Lord.

Priest: Lamb of God, Who takest away the sins of the world,

All: Have mercy on us.

Priest: Jesus meek and humble of Heart,

All: Make our hearts like unto Thine.

About the Author

Annabelle Moseley is an award-winning American poet, inventor of a new poetic form, the "mirror sonnet," Professor of Theology, and the author of eleven books including *Sacred Braille: The Rosary as Masterpiece through Art, Poetry and Reflections*, which has been honored as a Finalist for the 2020 Association of Catholic Publishers Awards in the category of Prayer. *Sacred Braille* has been transcribed into Braille through the Xavier Society for the Blind and made available for free to the visually impaired. Host of the Catholic podcasts on Sacramental Living: "Then Sings My Soul," and "Destination: Sainthood" on WCAT Radio, Moseley is also a recurring guest on Relevant Radio's "Morning Air," has appeared on Catholic Faith Network, and her work as a poet is featured as one of five artists profiled in the 2019 Documentary Film, *Masterpieces*, about the vocational call of the arts. The film is available to view through Amazon and Formed.org.

Made in United States
Orlando, FL
05 April 2022

16533028R00202